KS3 Phonics

Teacher Handbook

Introduction

The *Key Stage 3 Phonics Series* has been carefully designed to provide you with the materials you need to teach learners that have reached Key Stage 3 but are unable to read or write well enough to thrive with the demands of a Key Stage 3 curriculum. In some places this is thought to be as much as 60% of the Year 7 cohort.

In the introduction section of the *KS3 Phonics Student Workbooks*, learners are informed that learning to read and write in the English language is especially challenging. They are reassured that even proficient readers and writers have to work hard to get better at reading and writing.

Many people perceive phonics as something that is concluded in the infants. This is a misconception that we need to address. It causes older learners to face the challenge of low self-esteem alongside the difficulties of weak literacy skills. We do teach using phonics in the infants, but the English language takes many years to master. Even adults who are good readers and writers still use phonics if they need to read or spell a new or difficult word.

Phonics can be explained to learners as being similar to a spy code. Phonics is a code that matches the sounds that we make when we speak with the letters that we use when we read or write. For example, when you see the letter b you say /b/ as in bat. When you see the letters ee together you say /ee/ as in eel. The slash marks // mean sound. The letter c can be a /k/ sound as in cat, or a /s/ sound as in city.

There are over 150 pieces of code (letter/sound combinations, or grapheme/phoneme correspondences) in English so it is no great surprise that many learners struggle to master it during the first few years of school.

The content of this comprehensive course covers the English Alphabetic Code across one academic year. Each *KS3 Phonics Student Workbook* has 46 – 48 short, standalone lessons. If the learner is able to receive 1 x 20-minute lesson for 5 days a week, a workbook will be completed in ten weeks. All three workbooks can be completed within 30 weeks.

The lessons follow the same structure throughout the course. This eliminates the need for teachers to spend time explaining activities. Time is used efficiently by both teacher and learner to focus on the knowledge and skills being taught, practised and embedded. Many Key Stage 3 learners taking this course will have irregular gaps in their knowledge and skills. Some lessons will be new learning and some lessons will be revision.

Getting Started

How do I know which KS3 Phonics Student Workbook to use for my learners?

Use the *Diagnostic Assessment Sheet* to help you evaluate whether to place learners on *KS3 Phonics Student Workbook 1, 2* or *3*.

Using this assessment tool will give you a measurable baseline score which can be tracked for progress and can be used to evaluate impact.

How do I use the Diagnostic Assessment?

The Diagnostic Assessment in the Key Stage 3 Phonics series is a form of test known as a 'Stop Test'. This means that if a learner is not scoring well as the test progresses, the test is stopped, and the learner is not expected to continue to the end.

The Diagnostic Assessment has 3 sections. All learners complete Section 1. Learners who do not score highly, do not progress to Section 2. Those that do progress to Section 2 but do not score highly, do not progress to Section 3.

The Diagnostic Assessment needs to be conducted 1:1 but should only take a few minutes per learner.

Give the learner a copy of the *Diagnostic Assessment Student Sheet*.
The adult administering the test needs a copy of the *Diagnostic Assessment Teacher Sheet*.

1. Ask the learner to look at the graphemes (letters) in Section 1 and say the sound that each represents. You may need to give an example: "If you see the letter 's' you say /s/." Some of the graphemes represent more than one sound and either answer is acceptable. The *Diagnostic Assessment Teacher Sheet* indicates the possible sounds and provides you with key words to support your own knowledge of sounds. Each correct box equates to 1 mark, a total of 20.

2. Ask the learner to read each of the words in Section 1. If the word is a homophone e.g. 'tear', accept either pronunciation as correct. Each correct box equates to 1 mark, a total of 15.

3. Use the *Diagnostic Assessment Teacher Sheet* to dictate the words in Section 1 for the learner to write into the corresponding boxes. Each correct box equates to 1 mark, a total of 15.

Add the marks achieved in Section 1 together, up to a potential total of 50 marks.
If the learner scores less than 40, start them on *KS3 Phonics Student Workbook 1* and do not continue to conduct Section 2 of the *Diagnostic Assessment Sheet*.
If the learner scores 40 or more, continue to conduct Section 2 of the *Diagnostic Assessment Sheet*.

When the learner has completed Section 2 add together all of the marks from Section 1 and 2, up to a potential total of 100 marks.
If the learner scores less than 90, start them on *KS3 Phonics Student Workbook 2*.
If the learner scores 90 or more, continue to conduct Section 3 of the *Diagnostic Assessment Sheet*.

When the learner has completed Section 3 add together all of the marks from Sections 1, 2 and 3, up to a potential total of 150 marks.
If the learner scores less than 140, start them on *KS3 Phonics Student Workbook 3*.
If the learner scores 140 or more, the Key Stage 3 Phonics series is unlikely to be a necessary programme of work.

If in doubt start on a lower level workbook, and do not jump around within workbooks to plug gaps but work systematically from start to finish – revision lessons are still valuable additional practice.

Repeat the Diagnostic Assessment at the learners' exit point (when they have finished the series). This will give you a comparison score to measure progress accurately.

How can I track and monitor progress?

Use a copy of the class tracking sheet to keep a record of learners' baseline Diagnostic Assessment scores, their achievement at the end of each Workbook, and a repeat Diagnostic Assessment score at their point of exit from using the series.

KS3 Phonics Tracking Sheet

Student name	Diagnostic entry score	End of WB1 word assessment	End of WB2 word assessment	End of WB3 word assessment	Diagnostic exit score
Example A	25%	50%	75%	50%	60%
Example B	53%	n/a	80%	80%	75%
Example C	67%	n/a	n/a	90%	88%

At entry point/baseline all learners are regarded as achieving a score out of 150, irrelevant of whether they completed only Section 1, Sections 1 and 2 or all three sections. To convert the score to a percentage, use this equation:

(total score ÷ 150) X 100

For example, a learner with a total score of 36/150 has a percentage of 24%

$(36 \div 150) \times 100 = 24\%$

At the end of each *KS3 Phonics Student Workbook* there is a word level assessment. After completing the workbook, the learner takes the assessment by reading and spelling a selection of words at a level that matches the book content. This gives an indication of how well they have retained and are applying the content from each workbook. The score (marks out of 60) can be changed to a percentage using the equation: $(score \div 60) \times 100$

In *KS3 Phonics Student Workbooks 2* and *3* there is also a text level assessment. These assessments enable the teacher and the learner to check how well the learner is able to apply the content *beyond* word level. These formative text level assessments can be evaluated using teacher judgement.

Diagnostic Assessment Student Sheet				
Name:			Date:	
Section 1				

ck	u	ff	j	ai
oa	igh	ie	le	or
ea	ng	v	oo	y
th	ou	oy	er	ce
tint	skip	elf	juts	aid
flow	sigh	ton	snort	whisk
tongs	vast	took	bonny	chat

1.	2.	3.	4.	5.
6.	7.	8.	9.	10.
11.	12.	13.	14.	15.

Section 2

i-e	o-e	u-e	eer	ere
ier	ur	our	re	il
aw	al	oor	kn	dge
mn	sc	bu	rh	ti
gym	theme	fake	lair	tear
adhere	dirt	early	humour	brittle
numb	guide	chorus	chiffon	motion

1.	2.	3.	4.	5.
6.	7.	8.	9.	10.
11.	12.	13.	14.	15.

Total score (out of 100):

Diagnostic Assessment Student Sheet continued				
Name:			Date:	
Section 3				

gh	gn	eigh	ei	ui
eu	wa	gue	mn	ps
eau	ph	ssi	ous	aigh
ture	ie	al	que	iew
delusion	porous	gherkin	hasten	feign
paisley	heist	strewn	recoup	euphoria
haughty	chronic	quiche	oblique	pristine
1.	2.	3.	4.	5.
6.	7.	8.	9.	10.
11.	12.	13.	14.	15.
Total score (out of 150):				

Diagnostic Assessment Teacher Sheet (NB. The use of slash marks around a letter(s) like this /s/ indicates the sound and not the spelling)

/k/ (as in du**ck**)	/u/ (as in **u**mbrella)	/f/ (as in cli**ff**)	/j/ (as in **j**ump)	/ai/ (as in **ai**m)
/oa/ (as in b**oa**t)	/igh/ (as in n**igh**t)	/igh/ or /ee/ (as in p**ie** or f**ie**ld)	/ul/ (as in kett**le**)	/or/ (as in f**or**k)
/e/ or /ee/ or /ai/ (as in h**ea**d, b**ea**k or gr**ea**t)	/ng/ (as in ki**ng**)	/v/ (as in **v**iolin)	short or long /oo/ (as in b**oo**k or m**oo**n)	/y/ or /ee/ or /igh/ (as in **y**awn, happ**y** or sk**y**)
voiced or unvoiced /th/ (as in **th**is or **th**umb)	/ou/ (as in **ou**ch)	/oy/ (as in t**oy**)	/er/ (as in sist**er**)	/s/ (as in dan**ce**)
tint	skip	elf	juts	aid
flow	sigh	ton	snort	whisk
tongs	vast	took	bonny	chat
1. stray	2. soak	3. spied	4. cattle	5. freedom
6. zebra	7. team	8. buzz	9. link	10. love
11. stool	12. text	13. shall	14. quest	15. town
/igh/ (as in t**i**me)	/oa/ (as in r**o**pe)	/oo/ or /yoo/ (as in r**u**le or t**u**be)	/eer/ (as in d**eer**)	/air/ or /eer/ (as in wh**ere** or adh**ere**)
/eer/ (as in cash**ier**)	/er/ (as in n**ur**se)	/er/ or /or/ (as in hum**our** or f**our**)	/u/ (as in thea**tre**)	/ul/ (as in pen**cil**)
/or/ (as in y**aw**n)	/ul/ or /or/ (as in hospit**al** or cha**lk**)	/or/ (as in d**oor**)	/n/ (as in **kn**it)	/j/ (as in he**dge**)
/m/ (as in colu**mn**)	/s/ (as in **s**cissors)	/b/ (as in **b**uild)	/r/ (as in **rh**ino)	/sh/ (as in sta**ti**on)
gym	theme	fake	lair	tear
adhere	dirt	early	humour	brittle
numb	guide	chorus	chiffon	motion
1. circle	2. shine	3. throne	4. flute	5. care
6. there	7. fears	8. cashier	9. burnt	10. work
11. theatre	12. stencil	13. flannel	14. saucer	15. boar

Section 3

/g/ or /f/ (as in **gh**ost or lau**gh**)	/n/ (as in **gn**ome)	/ai/ (as in **eigh**t)	/igh/ or /ee/ (as in **ei**der or c**ei**ling)	/oo/ (as in fr**ui**t)
/yoo/ (as in f**eu**d)	/wo/ or /wor/ (as in **wa**tch or **wa**ter)	/g/ (as in catalo**gue**)	/m/ (as in colu**mn**)	/s/ (as in **ps**eudo)
/yoo/ or /oa/ (as in b**eau**ty or b**eau**)	/f/ (as in **ph**oto)	/sh/ (as in mi**ss**ion)	/us/ (as in curi**ous**)	/ai/ (as in str**aigh**t)
/chu/ (as in pic**ture**)	/igh/ or /ee/ (as in t**ie** or mov**ie**)	/or/ or /ol/ (as in w**al**k or s**al**t)	/k/ (as in che**que**)	/yoo/ (as in v**iew**)
delusion	porous	gherkin	hasten	feign
paisley	heist	strewn	recoup	euphoria
haughty	chronic	quiche	oblique	pristine
[1.]meagre	[2.]tableau	[3.]gesture	[4.]paltry	[5.]almond
[6.]psychology	[7.]solemn	[8.]cuisine	[9.]jasmine	[10.]define
[11.]rogue	[12.]quartet	[13.]brusque	[14.]mosquito	[15.]preview

Total score (out of 150):

KS3 Phonics Tracking Sheet

Student name	Diagnostic entry score	End of WB1 word assessment	End of WB2 word assessment	End of WB3 word assessment	Diagnostic exit score

Revisit and Review Charts

At the start of each *KS3 Phonics Student Workbook* are Revisit and Review Charts. These are used as a warm-up activity at the beginning of each lesson to help learners become confident in their knowledge of the alphabetic code.

As well as providing a practice and consolidation activity, they are a useful tool for learners' self-assessment. They are able to 'tick off' the code they know and take ownership over their own progression. They could do this using a different coloured pen at weekly or fortnightly intervals.

There are two specific skills that are rehearsed using the charts. Firstly, a sub-skill of reading: **see the letter/s and say the sound**. Learners independently, or with a partner, take turns to look at the graphemes (letters or letter groups) and say the sound that the grapheme represents. Sometimes the grapheme represents more than one sound. They key word underneath the grapheme helps the teacher and learner to identify the correct sound.

The second skill that is rehearsed using the charts is a sub-skill of spelling: **hear the sound and find the letter/s**. The teacher, or a partner, says a sound and the learner points to the corresponding grapheme on the chart.

Look at the letters and say the sounds: **Chart 1**

s	a	t	i
snake	apple	tent	insect
p	n	c	k
pan	net	cat	kit
ck	e	h	r
duck	egg	hat	rat
m	d	g	o
map	dig	girl	octopus
u	l	f	b
umbrella	ladder	feather	bat

Example of a Student Workbook 1 lesson

Introduction:

The letters s, a, t, i, p and n are code for the sound   and /n/.
There are other ways to spell some of these sound
Some of these letters can be more than one sound.
Today we are focusing on the simple code: 1 spelling for 1 so

Words used in the lesson that may be tricky

Remember to discuss the meanings of new or unusual words

1. Word reading. Read each word carefully. Tick it when yo

sat sit its nip pit at pin Nan tip tin

2. Dictation time. Listen carefully and write the 3 sentences your teacher tells you.

a)
_____   _____

Sentences are provided in this handbook or you could use your own ideas

b)
_____

c)
_____

3. Letter hunt. Find and underline all the 'a' and 'i' letters. Then read the text.

An ant nips in a tin.

The ant sits in the tin.

Pat tips the tin that the ant is in.

Ask questions to check understanding. For example, 'Who nips in a tin? Where does the ant sit? What does Pat do?'

4. Now it's your turn. Write 3 short sentences that include words with today's focus code.

a)
_____   _____

Support students who might need help to think of sentences

b)
_____

c)
_____

5. Challenge. Which of today's sounds can be spelled using different letters?

The purpose of the challenge is for the teacher to draw attention to details about the focus code

_____

_____

Lesson 1 c (e, i, y)

Example of a Student Workbook 2 lesson

Introduction:
The letter c can be code for the sound /s/ when it is followed by an e, i or y.
There are other ways to spell the sound /s/: s, -ss, -ce, -se, c (e, i, y), sc, -st- or ps.
Today we are focusing on the c (e, i, y) spelling of the /s/ sound.

1. Word reading. Read each word carefully. Tick it when you've read it.

city cents central cellar citrus cygnet cinema

2. Dicta   ells
you.

a)

- **Same format and structure as Student Workbook 1 lessons**
- **Subtle progression**
- **More complex alphabetic code – spelling alternatives**
- **More complex vocabulary**
- **Text for reading is slightly longer and has a slightly smaller font**

b)

c)

3. Letter hunt. Find and underline all the 'c' as /s/ code. Then read the text.

Cinderella lived in the cellar. She was a good citizen. She cooked and cleaned for her wicked step-sisters but she was never allowed out to the cinema or to the city. She felt certain that her circumstances held her back from success.

4. Now it's your turn. Write 3 short sentences that include words with today's focus code.

a)

b)

c)

5. Challenge. How do you know when the letter c may be an /s/ and not a /k/?

Lesson 1 ssi as in admission

Example of a Student Workbook 3 lesson

Introduction:
There are several graphemes which represent the /sh/ sound: sh, ch, -ti, -ci and -ssi.
Note that the end of every word is spelt -ssion and this word chunk is pronounced "shun".

1. Word reading. Read each word carefully. Tick it when you've read it.

mission   admission   permission   passion   expression
discussion   compassion   possession

2. Dicta

a)

b)

c)

- **Same format and structure as Student Workbook 1 and 2 lessons**
- **Subtle progression**
- **More complex alphabetic code – less common spelling alternatives**
- **More complex vocabulary**
- **Text for reading is longer and has a smaller font**
- **No challenge section**

3. Letter hunt. Find and underline all the 'ssi' as /sh/ code. Then read the text.

Sanjay and Sally had been given instructions for a new mission. The task was to take possession of a top-secret robot. They had a discussion with Mr Black (the department manager) and he gave them permission to get started. When they reached the hidden location of the robot, they gained admission to the site by showing fake IDs. "You may enter by proxy," said the gatekeeper. "What an odd expression," said Sanjay. "That gatekeeper didn't make any sense." "Show some compassion, Sanjay!" exclaimed Sally. "He's probably had that job for the last fifty years and has lost all passion for it." As Sally finished her sentence, Sanjay looked at her with wide eyes. Sally instantly knew what he was thinking. "The gatekeeper is a robot!" they said in unison.

4. Now it's your turn. Write 3 short sentences that include words with today's focus code.

a)

b)

c)

KS3 Phonics Student Workbook 1 Contents

Student Workbook 1 Lesson 1 Revising s, a, t, i, p, n   **the, that**

Warm up: Ask students to turn to the chart on page 4 and practise saying the sounds with a partner. One says the sounds in the shaded boxes, the other says the sounds in the white boxes, then swap.

Introduction: Explain to students that the letters s, a, t, i, p and n are code for the sounds /s/ /a/ /t/ /i/ /p/ and /n/. There are other ways to spell some of these sounds. Some of these letters can represent more than one sound. Today we are focusing on one spelling for one sound.

1. Word reading: Ask students to read each word carefully and tick to self-assess each word read. The words are *sat, sit, its, nip, pit, at, pin, Nan, tip* and *tin.* Discuss any new or unusual word meanings.

2. Dictation time: Ask students to listen carefully and then write each sentence that you dictate.
a) Nan tips the tin.   b) The ant nips as I pat it.   c) The pin is in the tin.

3. Letter hunt: Ask students to scan through the text carefully and underline all the 'a' and 'i' letters. Then they should read back through the text, this time reading for accuracy and meaning. Ask a question to check understanding, for example: *What did Pat do?*

4. Now it's your turn: Ask students to write three of their own short sentences using at least one word per sentence that contains today's focus code.

5. Challenge: Ask students to think about the challenge question. Draw attention to the knowledge that /a/ is the only sound in today's lesson that cannot be spelled a different way. All of the other sounds have different ways of being spelled. Refer to the English Alphabetic Code Chart at the end of the workbook to see this.

Student Workbook 1 Lesson 2 Revising c, k, ck, e, h   **the**

Warm up: Ask students to turn to the chart on page 4 and point to the letters that match the sounds you say. Call out a selection of sounds from Chart 1 at a brisk pace, allowing just enough time for learners to scan and point to the letters each time.

Introduction: Explain to students that the letters c, k, ck are all code for the sound /k/. The letters e and h are code for the sounds /e/ and /h/. Today we are focusing on three different ways to spell the /k/ sound and the simple spellings of /e/ and /h/.

1. Word reading: Ask students to read each word carefully and tick to self-assess each word read. The words are *cat, kit, skip, pick, peck, ten, hat, hens, hit* and *cap.* Discuss any new or unusual words.

2. Dictation time: Ask students to listen carefully and then write each sentence that you dictate.
a) The hen pecks a pan.   b) The kit has ten hats.   c) The cat naps in a cap.

3. Letter hunt: Ask students to scan through the text carefully and underline all the letters that are code for /k/ sound. Then they should read the text, this time reading for accuracy and meaning. Ask a question to check understanding, for example: *What type of animal is Ken?*

4. Now it's your turn: Ask students to write three of their own short sentences using at least one word per sentence that contains today's focus code.

5. Challenge: Ask students to think about the challenge question. Draw attention to the knowledge that the ck spelling of the /k/ sound isn't used at the beginning of words.

Warm up: Ask students to turn to the chart on page 4 and practise saying the sounds with a partner. One says the sounds in the shaded boxes, the other says the sounds in the white boxes, then swap.

Introduction: Explain to students that the letters r, m, d, g and o are code for the sounds /r/ /m/ /d/ /g/ and /o/. There are other ways to spell some of these sounds. Some of these letters can represent more than one sound. Today we are focusing on one spelling for one sound.

1. Word reading: Ask students to read each word carefully and tick to self-assess each word read. The words are *rat, rip, map, him, red, mad, get, peg, top* and *hot*. Discuss any new or unusual words.

2. Dictation time: Ask students to listen carefully and then write each sentence that you dictate.
a) I got hot and mad.   b) Tim had a rip in his top.   c) The rat got a map.

3. Letter hunt: Ask students to scan through the text carefully and underline all the 'd' and 'g' letters. Then they should read back through the text, this time reading for accuracy and meaning. Ask a question to check understanding, for example: *Where did Dan and his dog stop?*

4. Now it's your turn: Ask students to write three of their own short sentences using at least one word per sentence that contains today's focus code.

5. Challenge: Ask students to think about the challenge question. Draw attention to the knowledge that all of today's sounds can be spelled in multiple ways. Refer to the English Alphabetic Code Chart at the end of the workbook to see this.

Warm up: Ask students to turn to the chart on page 4 and point to the letters that match the sounds you say. Call out a selection of sounds from Chart 1 at a brisk pace, allowing just enough time for learners to scan and point to the letters each time.

Introduction: Explain to students that the letters u, l, b and f are code for the sounds /u/ /l/ /b/ and /f/. There are other ways to spell some of these sounds. Some of these letters can represent more than one sound. Today we are focusing on one spelling for one sound.

1. Word reading: Ask students to read each word carefully and tick to self-assess each word read. The words are *mud, gum, leg, luck, fog, fig, elf, bin, bag* and *grab*. Discuss any new or unusual words.

2. Dictation time: Ask students to listen carefully and then write each sentence that you dictate.
a) I grab a bag of figs.   b) The elf has mud on his leg.   c) Dad got stuck in the fog.

3. Letter hunt: Ask students to scan through the text carefully and underline all the 'u' and 'b' letters. Then they should read back through the text, this time reading for accuracy and meaning. Ask a question to check understanding, for example: *How did Fred trick his friends?*

4. Now it's your turn: Ask students to write three of their own short sentences using at least one word per sentence that contains today's focus code.

5. Challenge: Ask students to think about the challenge question. Draw attention to the knowledge that 'u' is the only letter in today's lesson that can represent more than one sound. The other letters on their own represent only one sound but combined into digraphs such as 'al', 'mb' represent different sounds. Refer to the English Alphabetic Code Chart at the end of the workbook to see this.

Warm up: Ask students to turn to the chart on page 4 and practise saying the sounds with a partner. One says the sounds in the shaded boxes, the other says the sounds in the white boxes, then swap.

Introduction: Explain to students that the letters ll, ff and ss are all code for the sounds /l/ /f/ and /s/. We only make one sound for double consonant letters. It is the same for: bb, rr, dd, gg, tt, mm, nn and zz. Today we are focusing on the double consonant letters: ll, ff and ss.

1. Word reading: Ask students to read each word carefully and tick to self-assess each word read. The words are *ill, tell, hill, cuff, huff, puff, off, less, fuss* and *miss*. Discuss any new or unusual word meanings.

2. Dictation time: Ask students to listen carefully and then write each sentence that you dictate.
a) Mud is on his cuffs.   b) Dan is in a huff.   c) Nell felt ill on the trip.

3. Letter hunt: Ask students to scan through the text carefully and underline all the double letters. Then they should read back through the text, this time reading for accuracy and meaning. Ask a question to check understanding, for example: *Why do you think Sid and Tim were huffing and puffing?*

4. Now it's your turn: Ask students to write three of their own short sentences using at least one word per sentence that contains today's focus code.

5. Challenge: Ask students to think about the challenge question. Example answers could include *bottle, little, skipping, stopped, swimming,* etc.

Student Workbook 1 Lesson 6 j as in jug   **the**

Warm up: Ask students to turn to the chart on page 4 and point to the letters that match the sound you say. Call out a selection of sounds from Chart 1 at a brisk pace, allowing just enough time for learners to scan and point to the letters each time.

Introduction: Explain to students that the letter j is code for the sound /j/ as in jug. There are other ways to spell the /j/ sound too. It can look like this: j, -dge, -ge or g (followed by e, i, or y). Today we are focusing on the j spelling of the /j/ sound.

1. Word reading: Ask students to read each word carefully and tick to self-assess each word read. The words are *jet, jam, jug, juts, jag, just, jump, jacket, jig* and *jog*. Discuss any new or unusual word meanings.

2. Dictation time: Ask students to listen carefully and then write each sentence that you dictate.
a) Jen jogs to get fit.   b) Jim has a jam bun.   c) The red jacket is in the bag.

3. Letter hunt: Ask students to scan through the text carefully and underline all the 'j' letters. Then they should read back through the text, this time reading for accuracy and meaning. Ask a question to check understanding, for example: *How did Jon and Jen get to Japan?*

4. Now it's your turn: Ask students to write three of their own short sentences using at least one word per sentence that contains today's focus code.

5. Challenge: Ask students to think about the challenge question. Draw attention to the knowledge that the letter 'j' is usually used at the beginning of words in the English language and rarely at the end. Examples of the letter 'j' used in the middle of words include *hijack* and *injury*.

Student Workbook 1 Lesson 7 y as in yawn the

Warm up: Ask students to turn to the chart on page 4 and practise saying the sounds with a partner. One says the sounds in the shaded boxes, the other says the sounds in the white boxes, then swap.

Introduction: Explain to students that the letter y is code for the sound /y/ as in yawn. The letter y can represent other sounds too. It can sound like /i/ in cymbals, /igh/ in shy, and /ee/ in happy. Today we are focusing on the y spelling of the /y/ sound.

1. Word reading: Ask students to read each word carefully and tick to self-assess each word read. The words are *yet, yen, yam, yak, yap, yell, yelp, yes* and *yum*. Discuss any new or unusual word meanings.

2. Dictation time: Ask students to listen carefully and then write each sentence that you dictate.
a) The yak yelps to get help.   b) The ticket cost ten yen.   c) I had a yam.

3. Letter hunt: Ask students to scan through the text carefully and underline all the 'y' letters. Then they should read back through the text, this time reading for accuracy and meaning. Ask a question to check understanding, for example: *Why do you think the pup was yapping?*

4. Now it's your turn: Ask students to write three of their own short sentences using at least one word per sentence that contains today's focus code.

5. Challenge: Ask students to think about the challenge question. Draw attention to the knowledge that the letter 'y' as a /y/ sound usually comes at the beginning of words whereas the letter 'y' as an /ee/ sound usually comes at the end of words e.g. happy, silly, funny.

Student Workbook 1 Lesson 8 ai as in aid the, to, he

Warm up: Ask students to turn to the chart on page 4 and point to the letters that match the sound you say. Call out a selection of sounds from Chart 1 at a brisk pace, allowing just enough time for learners to scan and point to the letters each time.

Introduction: Explain to students that the letters ai are code for the sound /ai/ as in aid. There are other ways to spell the /ai/ sound too. It can look like this: ai, ay, a, ae, a-e, ey, eigh, ea or aigh. Today we are focusing on the ai spelling of the /ai/ sound.

1. Word reading: Ask students to read each word carefully and tick to self-assess each word read. The words are *aim, aid, rail, pain, maid, fail, train* and *faint*. Discuss any new or unusual word meanings.

2. Dictation time: Ask students to listen carefully and then write each sentence that you dictate.
a) A snail was in the pail.   b) We went on a fun trail.   c) The postman left the mail.

3. Letter hunt: Ask students to scan through the text carefully and underline all the 'ai' letters. Then they should read back through the text, this time reading for accuracy and meaning. Ask a question to check understanding, for example: *Where was Emma going?*

4. Now it's your turn: Ask students to write three of their own short sentences using at least one word per sentence that contains today's focus code.

5. Challenge: Ask students to think about the challenge question. Draw attention to the knowledge that the 'ai' spelling of the /ai/ sound is usually used in the middle of words.

Warm up: Ask students to turn to the chart on page 4 and practise saying the sounds with a partner. One says the sounds in the shaded boxes, the other says the sounds in the white boxes, then swap.

Introduction: Explain to students that the letters ay are code for the /ai/ sound as in tray. There are other ways to spell the /ai/ sound too. It can look like this: ai, ay, a, ae, a-e, ey, eigh, ea or aigh. Today we are focusing on the ay spelling of the /ai/ sound.

1. Word reading: Ask students to read each word carefully and tick to self-assess each word read. The words are *day, say, may, pay, stray, crayon, stay* and *Sunday*. Discuss any new or unusual word meanings.

2. Dictation time: Ask students to listen carefully and then write each sentence that you dictate.
a) I lay in bed on Sundays.   b) I say it is a bad day.   c) A crayon fell on the tray.

3. Letter hunt: Ask students to scan through the text carefully and underline all the 'ay' letters. Then they should read back through the text, this time reading for accuracy and meaning. Ask a question to check understanding, for example: *What type of dog did Dad get?*

4. Now it's your turn: Ask students to write three of their own short sentences using at least one word per sentence that contains today's focus code.

5. Challenge: Ask students to think about the challenge question. Draw attention to the knowledge that the 'ay' spelling of the /ai/ sound is usually used at the end of words. However, crayon is an example of 'ay' in the middle of a word.

Warm up: Ask students to turn to the chart on page 4 and point to the letters that match the sound you say. Call out a selection of sounds from Chart 1 at a brisk pace, allowing just enough time for learners to scan and point to the letters each time.

Introduction: Explain to students that the letter w is code for the sound /w/ as in web. There are other ways to spell the /w/ sound too. It can look like this: w, wh or -u. Today we are focusing on the w spelling of the /w/ sound.

1. Word reading: Ask students to read each word carefully and tick to self-assess each word read. The words are *wet, web, wag, wig, win, went, wind* and *swims*. Discuss any new or unusual word meanings.

2. Dictation time: Ask students to listen carefully and then write each sentence that you dictate.
a) Mum has a red wig on.   b) The web got wet in the rain.   c) Willa went on a jog.

3. Letter hunt: Ask students to scan through the text carefully and underline all the 'w' letters. Then they should read back through the text, this time reading for accuracy and meaning. Ask a question to check understanding, for example: *When does Will swim?*

4. Now it's your turn: Ask students to write three of their own short sentences using at least one word per sentence that contains today's focus code.

5. Challenge: Ask students to think about the challenge question. Draw attention to the knowledge that the 'w' spelling of the /w/ sound is usually used at the beginning of words. When the letter 'w' is seen at the end of words it is often part of a digraph such as 'ow' which represents the /ow/ sound as in yellow.

Student Workbook 1 Lesson 11 oa as in oak   **the, this**

Warm up: Ask students to turn to the chart on page 4 and practise saying the sounds with a partner. One says the sounds in the shaded boxes, the other says the sounds in the white boxes, then swap.

Introduction: Explain to students that the letters oa are code for the sound /oa/ as in oak. There are other ways to spell the /oa/ sound too. It can look like this: oa, o, -oe, o-e, ow, -ough or eau. Today we are focusing on the oa spelling of the /oa/ sound.

1. Word reading: Ask students to read each word carefully and tick to self-assess each word read. The words are *oak, oats, coat, soak, boat, float, cloak* and *boast*. Discuss any new or unusual word meanings.

2. Dictation time: Ask students to listen carefully and then write each sentence that you dictate.
a) I soak the oats in milk.   b) I left a coat on the boat.   c) The goat naps next to the oak.

3. Letter hunt: Ask students to scan through the text carefully and underline all the 'oa' letters. Then they should read back through the text, this time reading for accuracy and meaning. Ask a question to check understanding, for example: *Why did the goat moan?*

4. Now it's your turn: Ask students to write three of their own short sentences using at least one word per sentence that contains today's focus code.

5. Challenge: Ask students to think about the challenge question. Draw attention to the knowledge that the 'oa' spelling of the /oa/ sound is usually used at the beginning and in the middle of words rather than at the end of words. The spelling 'ow' for the /oa/ sound is more common at the end of words.

Student Workbook 1 Lesson 12 ow as in own   **the**

Warm up: Ask students to turn to the chart on page 4 and point to the letters that match the sound you say. Call out a selection of sounds from Chart 1 at a brisk pace, allowing just enough time for learners to scan and point to the letters each time.

Introduction: Explain to students that the letters ow are code for the sound /oa/ as in own. There are other ways to spell the /oa/ sound too. It can look like this: oa, o, -oe, o-e, ow, -ough or eau. Today we are focusing on the ow spelling of the /oa/ sound.

1. Word reading: Ask students to read each word carefully and tick to self-assess each word read. The words are *own, low, snow, row, sow, crows, flow* and *grown*. Discuss any new or unusual word meanings.

2. Dictation time: Ask students to listen carefully and then write each sentence that you dictate.
a) I row the boat.   b) The dog has grown big.   c) Sanjay sows a row of bulbs.

3. Letter hunt: Ask students to scan through the text carefully and underline all the 'ow' letters. Then they should read back through the text, this time reading for accuracy and meaning. Ask a question to check understanding, for example: *Where did Joan get her crows from?*

4. Now it's your turn: Ask students to write three of their own short sentences using at least one word per sentence that contains today's focus code.

5. Challenge: Ask students to think about the challenge question. Draw attention to the knowledge that the letters 'ow' can represent the sound /oa/ as in own but can also represent the sound /ou/ as in flower. Refer to the English Alphabetic Code Chart at the end of the workbook to see this.

Student Workbook 1 Lesson 13 ie as in tie	this, the

Warm up: Ask students to turn to the chart on page 4 and practise saying the sounds with a partner. One says the sounds in the shaded boxes, the other says the sounds in the white boxes, then swap.

Introduction: Explain to students that the letters ie are code for the sound /igh/ as in tie. There are other ways to spell the /igh/ sound too. It can look like this: -igh, -ie, i, -y, i-e or ei. Today we are focusing on the ie spelling of the /igh/ sound.

1. Word reading: Ask students to read each word carefully and tick to self-assess each word read. The words are *lie, pie, tie, died, tried, spied, fried* and *denied*. Discuss any new or unusual word meanings.

2. Dictation time: Ask students to listen carefully and then write each sentence that you dictate.
a) Ted denied the lie.   b) Nick's pet fish died.   c) Anna tried to tie a bow.

3. Letter hunt: Ask students to scan through the text carefully and underline all the 'ie' letters. Then they should read back through the text, this time reading for accuracy and meaning. Ask a question to check understanding, for example: *Who made plum pie?*

4. Now it's your turn: Ask students to write three of their own short sentences using at least one word per sentence that contains today's focus code.

5. Challenge: Ask students to think about the challenge question. Draw attention to the knowledge that the letters 'ie' can represent the sound /igh/ as in tie but can also represent the sound /ee/ as in chief. Refer to the English Alphabetic Code Chart at the end of the workbook to see this.

Student Workbook 1 Lesson 14 igh as in night	the

Warm up: Ask students to turn to the chart on page 5 and practise saying the sounds with a partner. One says the sounds in the shaded boxes, the other says the sounds in the white boxes, then swap.

Introduction: Explain to students that the letters igh are code for the sound /igh/ as in night. There are other ways to spell the /igh/ sound too. It can look like this: -igh, -ie, i, -y, i-e or ei. Today we are focusing on the igh spelling of the /igh/ sound.

1. Word reading: Ask students to read each word carefully and tick to self-assess each word read. The words are *high, sigh, night, light, flight, slight, bright* and *tight*. Discuss any new or unusual word meanings.

2. Dictation time: Ask students to listen carefully and then write each sentence that you dictate.
a) The flight was at night.   b) The light is bright.   c) Helen's tight had a rip.

3. Letter hunt: Ask students to scan through the text carefully and underline all the 'igh' letters. Then they should read back through the text, this time reading for accuracy and meaning. Ask a question to check understanding, for example: *What gave Sanjay a fright?*

4. Now it's your turn: Ask students to write three of their own short sentences using at least one word per sentence that contains today's focus code.

5. Challenge: Ask students to think about the challenge question. Draw attention to the knowledge that the 'igh' spelling of the /igh/ sound is usually in the middle and at the end of words.

Student Workbook 1 Lesson 15 le as in kettle	**the, I, she**

Warm up: Ask students to turn to the chart on page 5 and point to the letters that match the sound you say. Call out a selection of sounds from Chart 2 at a brisk pace, allowing just enough time for learners to scan and point to the letters each time.

Introduction: Explain to students that the letters le are code for the sound /ul/ as in kettle. There are other ways to spell the /ul/ sound too. It can look like this: -le, -il, -al, -el. Today we are focusing on the le spelling of the /ul/ sound.

1. Word reading: Ask students to read each word carefully and tick to self-assess each word read. The words are *little, cattle, battle, middle, puddle, saddle* and *pickle*. Discuss any new or unusual word meanings.

2. Dictation time: Ask students to listen carefully and then write each sentence that you dictate.
a) The cattle sat in the middle of the road.   b) I fell off the saddle.   c) I had a little pickle.

3. Letter hunt: Ask students to scan through the text carefully and underline all the 'le' letters. Then they should read back through the text, this time reading for accuracy and meaning. Ask a question to check understanding, for example: *What did Karen spill?*

4. Now it's your turn: Ask students to write three of their own short sentences using at least one word per sentence that contains today's focus code.

5. Challenge: Ask students to think about the challenge question. Draw attention to the knowledge that the 'le' spelling of the /ul/ sound is usually at the end of words.

Student Workbook 1 Lesson 16 o as in son	**this, have**

Warm up: Ask students to turn to the chart on page 5 and practise saying the sounds with a partner. One says the sounds in the shaded boxes, the other says the sounds in the white boxes, then swap.

Introduction: Explain to students that the letter o can sometimes be code for the sound /u/ as in son. There are other ways to spell the /u/ sound too. It can look like this: u, o, -ou or -ough. Today we are focusing on the o spelling of the /u/ sound.

1. Word reading: Ask students to read each word carefully and tick to self-assess each word read. The words are *son, ton, front, Monday, London, some* and *done*. Ask students why they think the letters 'me' and 'ne' in some and done are underlined. Explain that we do not pronounce the end 'e' in these words. Discuss any new or unusual word meanings.

2. Dictation time: Ask students to listen carefully and then write each sentence that you dictate.
a) Monday is the best day.   b) I sat at the front of the train.   c) I went to London.

3. Letter hunt: Ask students to scan through the text carefully and underline all the 'o' as /u/ code. Then they should read back through the text, this time reading for accuracy and meaning. Ask a question to check understanding, for example: *Why did Jim go to London?*

4. Now it's your turn: Ask students to write three of their own short sentences using at least one word per sentence that contains today's focus code.

5. Challenge: Ask students to think about the challenge question. Draw attention to the knowledge that there are many words in the English language that end in a letter 'e' that we do not pronounce.

Student Workbook 1 Lesson 17 ee as in eel	to, he, no

Warm up: Ask students to turn to the chart on page 5 and point to the letters that match the sound you say. Call out a selection of sounds from Chart 2 at a brisk pace, allowing just enough time for learners to scan and point to the letters each time.

Introduction: Explain to students that the letters ee are code for the sound /ee/ as in eel. There are other ways to spell the /ee/ sound too. It can look like this: ee, e, e-e, ey, ie, ei, ea, y. Today we are focusing on the ee spelling of the /ee/ sound.

1. Word reading: Ask students to read each word carefully and tick to self-assess each word read. The words are *see, bee, meet, leek, green, freed, bleed* and *streets*. Discuss any new or unusual word meanings.

2. Dictation time: Ask students to listen carefully and then write each sentence that you dictate.
a) The bee sat on the tree.   b) We had green leeks.   c) We can meet on the street.

3. Letter hunt: Ask students to scan through the text carefully and underline all the 'ee' letters. Then they should read back through the text, this time reading for accuracy and meaning. Ask a question to check understanding, for example: *Who wants to feel free?*

4. Now it's your turn: Ask students to write three of their own short sentences using at least one word per sentence that contains today's focus code.

5. Challenge: Ask students to think about the challenge question. Draw attention to the knowledge that the ee spelling of the /e/ sound can be found anywhere in the word (e.g. *eel, meet, tree*) although it is less common at the beginning of words.

Student Workbook 1 Lesson 18 or as in fork	the, are

Warm up: Ask students to turn to the chart on page 5 and practise saying the sounds with a partner. One says the sounds in the shaded boxes, the other says the sounds in the white boxes, then swap.

Introduction: Explain to students that the letters or are code for the sound /or/ as in fork. There are other ways to spell the /or/ sound too. It can look like this: or, ore, oar, -oor, -our, (w)ar, aw, au, al, -augh or ough. Today we are focusing on the or spelling of the /or/ sound.

1. Word reading: Ask students to read each word carefully and tick to self-assess each word read. The words are *form, fork, torn, storm, stork, orbit, snort* and *fortress*. Discuss any new or unusual word meanings.

2. Dictation time: Ask students to listen carefully and then write each sentence that you dictate.
a) The fortress was a prison.   b) I bent the fork.   c) The storm has torn the hut.

3. Letter hunt: Ask students to scan through the text carefully and underline all the 'or' letters. Then they should read back through the text, this time reading for accuracy and meaning. Ask a question to check understanding, for example: *How bad do you think the storm was?*

4. Now it's your turn: Ask students to write three of their own short sentences using at least one word per sentence that contains today's focus code.

5. Challenge: Ask students to think about the challenge question. Draw attention to the knowledge that the or spelling for the /or/ sound can occur anywhere in the word (*orbit, fork, for*) but is more common in the middle of words.

Student Workbook 1 Lesson 19 z, zz as in zebra and jazz	**the, they, to, with**

Warm up: Ask students to turn to the chart on page 5 and point to the letters that match the sound you say. Call out a selection of sounds from Chart 2 at a brisk pace, allowing just enough time for learners to scan and point to the letters each time.

Introduction: Explain to students that the letters z and zz are code for the sound /z/ as in zebra and jazz. There are other ways to spell the /z/ sound too. It can look like this: z, -zz, -s, -se or -ze. Today we are focusing on the z and zz spellings of the /z/ sound.

1. Word reading: Ask students to read each word carefully and tick to self-assess each word read. The words are *zip, zest, zebra, fizz, jazz, buzz, frizz* and *zig-zag*. Discuss any new or unusual word meanings.

2. Dictation time: Ask students to listen carefully and then write each sentence that you dictate.
a) I play in a jazz band.   b) The zebra ran away.   c) The bee zips from tree to tree.

3. Letter hunt: Ask students to scan through the text carefully and underline all the 'z' and 'zz' letters. Then they should read back through the text, this time reading for accuracy and meaning. Ask a question to check understanding, for example: *What were the zebras' names?*

4. Now it's your turn: Ask students to write three of their own short sentences using at least one word per sentence that contains today's focus code.

5. Challenge: Ask students to think about the challenge question. Draw attention to the knowledge that the zz spelling of the /z/ sound doesn't occur at the beginning or words.

Student Workbook 1 Lesson 20 wh as in wheel	**the, they**

Warm up: Ask students to turn to the chart on page 5 and practise saying the sounds with a partner. One says the sounds in the shaded boxes, the other says the sounds in the white boxes, then swap.

Introduction: Explain to students that the letters wh are code for the sound /w/ as in wheel. There are other ways to spell the /w/ sound too. It can look like this: w, wh or -u. Today we are focusing on the wh spelling of the /w/ sound.

1. Word reading: Ask students to read each word carefully and tick to self-assess each word read. The words are *when, whip, wheel, whisk, whack, whiff* and *whiskers*. Discuss any new or unusual word meanings.

2. Dictation time: Ask students to listen carefully and then write each sentence that you dictate.
a) I went on the big wheel.   b) The cat has whiskers.   c) I gag when I whiff eggs.

3. Letter hunt: Ask students to scan through the text carefully and underline all the 'wh' letters. Then they should read back through the text, this time reading for accuracy and meaning. Ask a question to check understanding, for example: *What was wrong with the wheel?*

4. Now it's your turn: Ask students to write three of their own short sentences using at least one word per sentence that contains today's focus code.

5. Challenge: Ask students to think about the challenge question. Draw attention to the knowledge that the wh spelling of the /w/ sound is usually at the beginning of words.

Student Workbook 1 Lesson 21 ea as in eat	**she, the**

Warm up: Ask students to turn to the chart on page 5 and point to the letters that match the sound you say. Call out a selection of sounds from Chart 2 at a brisk pace, allowing just enough time for learners to scan and point to the letters each time.

Introduction: Explain to students that the letters ea are code for the sound /ee/ as in eat. There are other ways to spell the /ee/ sound too. It can look like this: ee, e, e-e, ey, ie, ei, ea or y. Today we are focusing on the ea spelling of the /ee/ sound.

1. Word reading: Ask students to read each word carefully and tick to self-assess each word read. The words are *eat, sea, team, heat, mean, feat, stream* and *scream*. Discuss any new or unusual word meanings.

2. Dictation time: Ask students to listen carefully and then write each sentence that you dictate.
a) Kim was picked to be in the team.   b) I dipped my feet in the stream.   c) Stan is a mean man.

3. Letter hunt: Ask students to scan through the text carefully and underline all the 'ea' letters. Then they should read back through the text, this time reading for accuracy and meaning. Ask a question to check understanding, for example: *What did Jean eat?*

4. Now it's your turn: Ask students to write three of their own short sentences using at least one word per sentence that contains today's focus code.

5. Challenge: Ask students to think about the challenge question. Draw attention to the knowledge that the ea spelling for the /ee/ sound can occur anywhere in the word (*eat, team, sea*) but is more common in the middle of words.

Student Workbook 1 Lesson 22 ea as in head

Warm up: Ask students to turn to the chart on page 5 and practise saying the sounds with a partner. One says the sounds in the shaded boxes, the other says the sounds in the white boxes, then swap.

Introduction: Explain to students that the letters ea can also be code for the sound /e/ as in head. There are other ways to spell the /e/ sound. It can look like this: e, -ea or -ai. Today we are focusing on the ea spelling of the /e/ sound.

1. Word reading: Ask students to read each word carefully and tick to self-assess each word read. The words are *head, instead, bread, lead, spread, dead* and *dreadful*. Discuss any new or unusual word meanings.

2. Dictation time: Ask students to listen carefully and then write each sentence that you dictate.
a) I spread jam on the bread.   b) The film was dreadful.   c) Can we go to the park instead?

3. Letter hunt: Ask students to scan through the text carefully and underline all the 'ea' letters. Then they should read back through the text, this time reading for accuracy and meaning. Ask a question to check understanding, for example: *How did Anne feel?*

4. Now it's your turn: Ask students to write three of their own short sentences using at least one word per sentence that contains today's focus code.

5. Challenge: Ask students to think about the challenge question. Draw attention to the knowledge that the letters 'ea' can represent the sound /e/ as in head but can also represent the sounds /ee/ as in eat and /ai/ as in break. Refer to the English Alphabetic Code Chart at the end of the workbook to see this.

Student Workbook 1 Lesson 23 /zh/ spelling alternatives	the, by, he

Warm up: Ask students to turn to the chart on page 5 and point to the letters that match the sound you say. Call out a selection of sounds from Chart 2 at a brisk pace, allowing just enough time for learners to scan and point to the letters each time.

Introduction: Explain to students that the letter z is code for the sound /z/ as in zebra. There are other ways to spell the /z/ sound. It can look like this: z, -zz, -s, -se or -ze. Today we are focusing on all the ways to spell the /z/ sound.

1. Word reading: Ask students to read each word carefully and tick to self-assess each word read. The words are *zip, buzz, is, was, fleas, tries, sneeze* and *please*. Discuss any new or unusual word meanings.

2. Dictation time: Ask students to listen carefully and then write each sentence that you dictate.
a) My cat had fleas.   b) The zip was stuck.   c) Gran likes to eat cheese.

3. Letter hunt: Ask students to scan through the text carefully and underline all the letters that are code for /z/ sound. Then they should read the text, this time reading for accuracy and meaning. Ask a question to check understanding, for example: *Where was Tom?*

4. Now it's your turn: Ask students to write three of their own short sentences using at least one word per sentence that contains today's focus code.

5. Challenge: Ask students to think about the challenge question. Explain that, like much of the English language, there are no exact rules but generally, if the word ends in a vowel or other voiced sound like /m/, /n/, /ng/, /l/, /b/, /d/, /g/, /v/, voiced /th/, or /r/ then the s or se will be pronounced as /z/. If the word ends in a voiceless sound like /p/, /t/, /k/, /f/ or voiceless /th/ the s or se will be pronounced /s/. If time permits investigate whether you find this to be true or not by looking at and saying different words ending in s and se.

Student Workbook 1 Lesson 24 ng as in gong	the, she

Warm up: Ask students to turn to the chart on page 5 and practise saying the sounds with a partner. One says the sounds in the shaded boxes, the other says the sounds in the white boxes, then swap.

Introduction: Explain to students that the letters ng are code for the sound /ng/ as in gong. In a few words, where the letters n and g are together, the letter n is code for /ng/ and g is sounded out, like in jungle (/j/ /u/ /ng/ /g/ /ul/). Today we are focusing on the ng spelling of the /ng/ sound.

1. Word reading: Ask students to read each word carefully and tick to self-assess each word read. The words are *hang, long, sing, wings, tongs, string, bring* and *swings*. Discuss any new or unusual word meanings.

2. Dictation time: Ask students to listen carefully and then write each sentence that you dictate.
a) We sang a long song.   b) The bug had big wings.   c) Please bring a bag of sweets.

3. Letter hunt: Ask students to scan through the text carefully and underline all the 'ng' letters. Then they should read back through the text, this time reading for accuracy and meaning. Ask a question to check understanding, for example: *What is Miss Wing good at doing?*

4. Now it's your turn: Ask students to write three of their own short sentences using at least one word per sentence that contains today's focus code.

5. Challenge: Ask students to think about the challenge question. Draw attention to the knowledge that the ng spelling of the /ng/ sound is usually at the end of words and is sometimes in the middle. It is not used at the beginning of words.

Student Workbook 1 Lesson 25 nk as in ink	the, he, to

Warm up: Ask students to turn to the chart on page 5 and point to the letters that match the sound you say. Call out a selection of sounds from Chart 2 at a brisk pace, allowing just enough time for learners to scan and point to the letters each time.

Introduction: Explain to students that the letters nk are code for the sound /ng+k/ as in ink. The sound /ng+k/ is actually two sounds /ng/ and /k/ but it is useful for reading and spelling to learn as one sound unit. Today we are focusing on the nk spelling of the /ng+k/ sound.

1. Word reading: Ask students to read each word carefully and tick to self-assess each word read. The words are *ink, sank, pink, tank, link, winks, stink* and *blanket*. Discuss any new or unusual word meanings.

2. Dictation time: Ask students to listen carefully and then write each sentence that you dictate.
a) I blink and look up.   b) The pot seemed to shrink.   c) I keep thinking of my big plan.

3. Letter hunt: Ask students to scan through the text carefully and underline all the 'nk' letters. Then they should read back through the text, this time reading for accuracy and meaning. Ask a question to check understanding, for example: *What colour was Hank's blanket?*

4. Now it's your turn: Ask students to write three of their own short sentences using at least one word per sentence that contains today's focus code.

5. Challenge: Ask students to think about the challenge question. Draw attention to the knowledge that the nk spelling of the /ng+k/ sound is usually at the end of words and is sometimes in the middle. It is not used at the beginning of words.

Student Workbook 1 Lesson 26 v as in violin	to, the

Warm up: Ask students to turn to the chart on page 5 and practise saying the sounds with a partner. One says the sounds in the shaded boxes, the other says the sounds in the white boxes, then swap.

Introduction: Explain to students that the letter v is code for the sound /v/ as in violin. There are two ways to spell the /v/ sound: v or -ve. Today we are focusing on the v spelling of the /v/ sound.

1. Word reading: Ask students to read each word carefully and tick to self-assess each word read. The words are *vet, van, vest, vast, vent, visit, invented* and *vat*. Discuss any new or unusual word meanings.

2. Dictation time: Ask students to listen carefully and then write each sentence that you dictate.
a) The victim slept at last.   b) A vixen sits next to the tree.   c) The vent let in a breeze.

3. Letter hunt: Ask students to scan through the text carefully and underline all the 'v' letters. Then they should read back through the text, this time reading for accuracy and meaning. Ask a question to check understanding, for example: *Where did Vik go?*

4. Now it's your turn: Ask students to write three of their own short sentences using at least one word per sentence that contains today's focus code.

5. Challenge: Ask students to think about the challenge question. Draw attention to the knowledge that the v spelling of the /v/ sound is usually at the beginning or middle of words. It is very rarely used at the end of words (*chav, spiv*).

Student Workbook 1 Lesson 27 ve as in dove	to, I, the, go

Warm up: Ask students to turn to the chart on page 5 and point to the letters that match the sound you say. Call out a selection of sounds from Chart 2 at a brisk pace, allowing just enough time for learners to scan and point to the letters each time.

Introduction: Explain to students that the letters ve are code for the sound /v/ as in dove. There are two ways to spell the /v/ sound: v or -ve. Today we are focusing on the ve spelling of the /v/ sound.

1. Word reading: Ask students to read each word carefully and tick to self-assess each word read. The words are *have, give, live, love, dove, above, glove* and *solve*. Discuss any new or unusual word meanings.

2. Dictation time: Ask students to listen carefully and then write each sentence that you dictate.
a) Shove the junk in the bag.   b) My plan will evolve.   c) Can you solve the problem?

3. Letter hunt: Ask students to scan through the text carefully and underline all the 've' letters. Then they should read back through the text, this time reading for accuracy and meaning. Ask a question to check understanding, for example: *How did Frank feel about the doves?*

4. Now it's your turn: Ask students to write three of their own short sentences using at least one word per sentence that contains today's focus code.

5. Challenge: Ask students to think about the challenge question. Draw attention to the knowledge that the ve spelling of the /v/ sound is used at the end of words. It is not used at the beginning of words.

Student Workbook 1 Lesson 28 oo as in book	the, he, to

Warm up: Ask students to turn to the chart on page 5 and practise saying the sounds with a partner. One says the sounds in the shaded boxes, the other says the sounds in the white boxes, then swap.

Introduction: Explain to students that the letters oo are code the sound short /oo/ as in book. There are other ways to spell the short /oo/ sound: -oo, -oul or -u. Today we are focusing on the oo spelling of the short /oo/ sound.

1. Word reading: Ask students to read each word carefully and tick to self-assess each word read. The words are *look, good, took, hood, rooks, stood, crook* and *nook*. Discuss any new or unusual word meanings.

2. Dictation time: Ask students to listen carefully and then write each sentence that you dictate.
a) We stood on top of the hill.   b) Gran has a crooked stick.   c) I shook my head.

3. Letter hunt: Ask students to scan through the text carefully and underline all the 'oo' letters. Then they should read back through the text, this time reading for accuracy and meaning. Ask a question to check understanding, for example: *What looked at Nick?*

4. Now it's your turn: Ask students to write three of their own short sentences using at least one word per sentence that contains today's focus code.

5. Challenge: Ask students to think about the challenge question. Draw attention to the knowledge that the oo spelling of the short /oo/ sound is usually used in the middle of words. It is not used at the beginning of words.

Student Workbook 1 Lesson 29 oo as in moon	**the**

Warm up: Ask students to turn to the chart on page 5 and point to the letters that match the sound you say. Call out a selection of sounds from Chart 2 at a brisk pace, allowing just enough time for learners to scan and point to the letters each time.

Introduction: Explain to students that the letters oo can also be used for the sound long /oo/ as in moon. There are other ways to spell the long /oo/ sound: oo, u-e, -ew, -ui, -ou, -o or -ue. Today we are focusing on the oo spelling of the long /oo/ sound.

1. Word reading: Ask students to read each word carefully and tick to self-assess each word read. The words are *pool, cool, mood, food, tools, stool, spoon* and *roof*. Discuss any new or unusual word meanings.

2. Dictation time: Ask students to listen carefully and then write each sentence that you dictate.
a) The rocket went zoom. b) I cleaned my room. c) The train went 'toot, toot!'

3. Letter hunt: Ask students to scan through the text carefully and underline all the 'oo' letters. Then they should read back through the text, this time reading for accuracy and meaning. Ask a question to check understanding, for example: *What did the moon do?*

4. Now it's your turn: Ask students to write three of their own short sentences using at least one word per sentence that contains today's focus code.

5. Challenge: Ask students to think about the challenge question. Draw attention to the knowledge that the oo spelling of the short /oo/ sound is most often used in the middle of words.

Student Workbook 1 Lesson 30 y as in sunny	**he, to, the, be**

Warm up: Ask students to turn to the chart on page 5 and practise saying the sounds with a partner. One says the sounds in the shaded boxes, the other says the sounds in the white boxes, then swap.

Introduction: Explain to students that the letter y is code for the sound /ee/ as in sunny. Some accents mean people pronounce this sound more like an /i/. This sound can also be spelled in these ways: -y, -ey or -ie. Today we are focusing on the y spelling of the /ee/ sound.

1. Word reading: Ask students to read each word carefully and tick to self-assess each word read. The words are *happy, funny, bonny, tummy, sleepy* and *gloomy*. Discuss any new or unusual word meanings.

2. Dictation time: Ask students to listen carefully and then write each sentence that you dictate.
a) I feel grumpy. b) The paint is sloppy and drippy. c) That cheese is smelly.

3. Letter hunt: Ask students to scan through the text carefully and underline all the 'y' letters. Then they should read back through the text, this time reading for accuracy and meaning. Ask a question to check understanding, for example: *Why do you think Billy was happy?*

4. Now it's your turn: Ask students to write three of their own short sentences using at least one word per sentence that contains today's focus code.

5. Challenge: Ask students to think about the challenge question. Draw attention to the knowledge that the y spelling of the /ee/ sound is used at the end of words.

Student Workbook 1 Lesson 31 x as in fox	to, the, with

Warm up: Ask students to turn to the chart on page 5 and point to the letters that match the sound you say. Call out a selection of sounds from Chart 2 at a brisk pace, allowing just enough time for learners to scan and point to the letters each time.

Introduction: Explain to students that the letter x is code for the sound /k+s/ as in fox. The sound /k+s/ is actually two sounds /k/ and /s/ but it is useful for reading and spelling to learn as one sound unit. Today we are focusing on the x spelling of the /k+s/ sound.

1. Word reading: Ask students to read each word carefully and tick to self-assess each word read. The words are *ox, fox, box, fix, six, text, maximum, relax* and *mixing*. Discuss any new or unusual word meanings.

2. Dictation time: Ask students to listen carefully and then write each sentence that you dictate.
a) I like to relax with a cup of tea.   b) I sent a text to my mum.   c) Six foxes sat in a box.

3. Letter hunt: Ask students to scan through the text carefully and underline all the 'x' letters. Then they should read back through the text, this time reading for accuracy and meaning. Ask a question to check understanding, for example: *Where do the foxes get food from?*

4. Now it's your turn: Ask students to write three of their own short sentences using at least one word per sentence that contains today's focus code.

5. Challenge: Ask students to think about the challenge question. Draw attention to the knowledge that the x spelling of the /k+s/ sound is used in the middle and at the end of words. It is not used at the beginning of words.

Student Workbook 1 Lesson 32 ch as in chair	with, the, they

Warm up: Ask students to turn to the chart on page 5 and practise saying the sounds with a partner. One says the sounds in the shaded boxes, the other says the sounds in the white boxes, then swap.

Introduction: Explain to students that the letters ch are code for the sound /ch/ as in chair. There are other ways to spell the /ch/ sound: ch, -tch or sometimes -ture. (-ture is close to /ch+u/). Today we are focusing on the ch spelling of the /ch/ sound.

1. Word reading: Ask students to read each word carefully and tick to self-assess each word read. The words are *chips, chat, such, rich, chick, lunch, inches* and *pinch*. Discuss any new or unusual word meanings.

2. Dictation time: Ask students to listen carefully and then write each sentence that you dictate.
a) I had a chat with Bill.   b) Mum chops the carrots.   c) We got a bunch of bananas.

3. Letter hunt: Ask students to scan through the text carefully and underline all the 'ch' letters. Then they should read back through the text, this time reading for accuracy and meaning. Ask a question to check understanding, for example: *Where did Chad and Rich have lunch?*

4. Now it's your turn: Ask students to write three of their own short sentences using at least one word per sentence that contains today's focus code.

5. Challenge: Ask students to think about the challenge question. Draw attention to the knowledge that the ch spelling of the /ch/ sound is used at the beginning, in the middle and at the end of words.

Student Workbook 1 Lesson 33 sh as in sheep	to, the, she

Warm up: Ask students to turn to the chart on page 5 and point to the letters that match the sound you say. Call out a selection of sounds from Chart 2 at a brisk pace, allowing just enough time for learners to scan and point to the letters each time.

Introduction: Explain to students that the letters sh are code for the /sh/ sound as in sheep. There are other ways to spell the /sh/ sound: sh, ch, -ti, -ci or -ssi. Today we are focusing on the sh spelling of the /sh/ sound.

1. Word reading: Ask students to read each word carefully and tick to self-assess each word read. The words are *ship, bash, shop, rush, shelf, brush, splash* and *shall*. Discuss any new or unusual word meanings.

2. Dictation time: Ask students to listen carefully and then write each sentence that you dictate.
a) I collect seashells.   b) The sheep is resting.   c) Dad was in a rush.

3. Letter hunt: Ask students to scan through the text carefully and underline all the 'sh' letters. Then they should read back through the text, this time reading for accuracy and meaning. Ask a question to check understanding, for example: *What was Shelby doing?*

4. Now it's your turn: Ask students to write three of their own short sentences using at least one word per sentence that contains today's focus code.

5. Challenge: Ask students to think about the challenge question. Draw attention to the knowledge that the sh spelling of the /sh/ sound is used at the beginning, in the middle and at the end of words.

Student Workbook 1 Lesson 34 th as in thistle and there

Warm up: Ask students to turn to the chart on page 6 and practise saying the sounds with a partner. One says the sounds in the shaded boxes, the other says the sounds in the white boxes, then swap.

Introduction: Explain to students that the letters th are code for the sounds unvoiced /th/ as in thistle and voiced /th/ as in there. Try not to make a /f/ or /v/ sound when you read words with th. Today we are focusing on the th spelling of the /th/ sounds.

1. Word reading: Ask students to read each word carefully and tick to self-assess each word read. The words are *thin, moth, this, that, then, the, thanks* and *three*. Discuss any new or unusual word meanings.

2. Dictation time: Ask students to listen carefully and then write each sentence that you dictate.
a) This is the best lesson.   b) I sat in a hot bath.   c) We ran up the path.

3. Letter hunt: Ask students to scan through the text carefully and underline all the 'th' letters. Then they should read back through the text, this time reading for accuracy and meaning. Ask a question to check understanding, for example: *What did Beth do?*

4. Now it's your turn: Ask students to write three of their own short sentences using at least one word per sentence that contains today's focus code.

5. Challenge: Ask students to think about the challenge question. The voiced /th/ words are: this, that, then, the. The unvoiced /th/ words are: thin, moth, thanks, three, thick, thistles, path, Beth, thumps, smooth, thrilling, maths.

Student Workbook 1 Lesson 35 qu as in queen	**her, she**

Warm up: Ask students to turn to the chart on page 6 and point to the letters that match the sound you say. Call out a selection of sounds from Chart 3 at a brisk pace, allowing just enough time for learners to scan and point to the letters each time.

Introduction: Explain to students that the letters qu are code for the sound /k+w/ as in queen. The sound /k+w/ is actually two sounds /k/ and /w/ but it is useful for reading and spelling to learn as one sound unit. Today we are focusing on the qu spelling of the /k+w/ sound.

1. Word reading: Ask students to read each word carefully and tick to self-assess each word read. The words are *quit, queen, quiz, quick, quest, squid* and *squirrel*. Discuss any new or unusual word meanings.

2. Dictation time: Ask students to listen carefully and then write each sentence that you dictate.
a) My boots squelched in the mud.   b) Squirrels eat nuts.   c) I will win the big quiz.

3. Letter hunt: Ask students to scan through the text carefully and underline all the 'qu' letters. Then they should read the text, this time reading for accuracy and meaning. Ask a question to check understanding, for example: *What did Queen Zelda squeeze?*

4. Now it's your turn: Ask students to write three of their own short sentences using at least one word per sentence that contains today's focus code.

5. Challenge: Ask students to think about the challenge question. Draw attention to the knowledge that the qu spelling of the /k+w/ sound isn't used at the end of words.

Student Workbook 1 Lesson 36 ou as in ouch	**he, to**

Warm up: Ask students to turn to the chart on page 6 and practise saying the sounds with a partner. One says the sounds in the shaded boxes, the other says the sounds in the white boxes, then swap.

Introduction: Explain to students that the letters ou are code for the sound /ou/ as in ouch. There are other ways to spell the /ou/ sound: ou, ow or -ough. Today we are focusing on the ou spelling of the /ou/ sound.

1. Word reading: Ask students to read each word carefully and tick to self-assess each word read. The words are *out, our, shout, mouth, south, proud* and *mountain*. Discuss any new or unusual word meanings.

2. Dictation time: Ask students to listen carefully and then write each sentence that you dictate.
a) My sister is loud.   b) A trout is a fish.   c) A hound is a dog.

3. Letter hunt: Ask students to scan through the text carefully and underline all the 'ou' letters. Then they should read back through the text, this time reading for accuracy and meaning. Ask a question to check understanding, for example: *What did the hound find?*

4. Now it's your turn: Ask students to write three of their own short sentences using at least one word per sentence that contains today's focus code.

5. Challenge: Ask students to think about the challenge question. Draw attention to the knowledge that the ou spelling of the /ou/ sound isn't used at the end of words.

Student Workbook 1 Lesson 37 ow as in owl	**her, she, to**

Warm up: Ask students to turn to the chart on page 6 and point to the letters that match the sound you say. Call out a selection of sounds from Chart 3 at a brisk pace, allowing just enough time for learners to scan and point to the letters each time.

Introduction: Explain to students that the letters ow are also code for the sound /ou/ as in owl. There are other ways to spell the /ou/ sound: ou, ow or -ough. Today we are focusing on the ow spelling of the /ou/ sound.

1. Word reading: Ask students to read each word carefully and tick to self-assess each word read. The words are *owl, now, how, down, town, crown, drown* and *frown*. Discuss any new or unusual word meanings.

2. Dictation time: Ask students to listen carefully and then write each sentence that you dictate.
a) The dog growled at the man.   b) The clown fell off the ladder.   c) I packed a towel in my bag.

3. Letter hunt: Ask students to scan through the text carefully and underline all the 'ow' letters. Then they should read back through the text, this time reading for accuracy and meaning. Ask a question to check understanding, for example: *Where did the owl land?*

4. Now it's your turn: Ask students to write three of their own short sentences using at least one word per sentence that contains today's focus code.

5. Challenge: Ask students to think about the challenge question. Draw attention to the knowledge that the ow spelling of the /ou/ sound is used at the beginning, in the middle and at the end of words.

Student Workbook 1 Lesson 38 oi as in ointment	**she**

Warm up: Ask students to turn to the chart on page 6 and practise saying the sounds with a partner. One says the sounds in the shaded boxes, the other says the sounds in the white boxes, then swap.

Introduction: Explain to students that the letters oi are code for the sound /oi/ as in ointment. There are other ways to spell the /oi/ sound: oi or oy. Today we are focusing on the oi spelling of the /oi/ sound.

1. Word reading: Ask students to read each word carefully and tick to self-assess each word read. The words are *oil, coin, join, soil, boil, point, joint, spoil* and *avoid*. Discuss any new or unusual word meanings.

2. Dictation time: Ask students to listen carefully and then write each sentence that you dictate.
a) Helen has ten coins in her pocket.   b) A splash of oil can spoil fabric.   c) Ken pointed at the void.

3. Letter hunt: Ask students to scan through the text carefully and underline all the 'oi' letters. Then they should read back through the text, this time reading for accuracy and meaning. Ask a question to check understanding, for example: *Why did Moira avoid joining in?*

4. Now it's your turn: Ask students to write three of their own short sentences using at least one word per sentence that contains today's focus code.

5. Challenge: Ask students to think about the challenge question. Draw attention to the knowledge that the oi spelling of the /oi/ sound isn't used at the end of words.

Student Workbook 1 Lesson 39 oy as in toy	to, he, they, are

Warm up: Ask students to turn to the chart on page 6 and point to the letters that match the sound you say. Call out a selection of sounds from Chart 3 at a brisk pace, allowing just enough time for learners to scan and point to the letters each time.

Introduction: Explain to students that the letters oy are also code for the sound /oi/ as in toy. There are other ways to spell the /oi/ sound: oi or oy. Today we are focusing on the oy spelling of the /oi/ sound.

1. Word reading: Ask students to read each word carefully and tick to self-assess each word read. The words are *loyal, coy, enjoy, decoy, destroy, royal* and *annoy*. Discuss any new or unusual word meanings.

2. Dictation time: Ask students to listen carefully and then write each sentence that you dictate.
a) I enjoy playing sports.   b) My sister annoys me.   c) I have a big oyster shell.

3. Letter hunt: Ask students to scan through the text carefully and underline all the 'oy' letters. Then they should read back through the text, this time reading for accuracy and meaning. Ask a question to check understanding, for example: *Why did Roy try to destroy toys?*

4. Now it's your turn: Ask students to write three of their own short sentences using at least one word per sentence that contains today's focus code.

5. Challenge: Ask students to think about the challenge question. Draw attention to the knowledge that the oy spelling of the /oi/ sound is used at the beginning, in the middle and at the end of words.

Student Workbook 1 Lesson 40 ue as in statue and blue

Warm up: Ask students to turn to the chart on page 6 and practise saying the sounds with a partner. One says the sounds in the shaded boxes, the other says the sounds in the white boxes, then swap.

Introduction: Explain to students that the letters ue are code for the sounds /y+oo/ as in statue and /oo/ as in blue. There are also other ways to spell these sounds: -ue, u-e or -ew. Today we are focusing on the ue spelling of the /y+oo/ and /oo/ sounds.

1. Word reading: Ask students to read each word carefully and tick to self-assess each word read. The words are *cue, hue, fuel, argue, rescue, true, clue* and *accrue*. Discuss any new or unusual word meanings.

2. Dictation time: Ask students to listen carefully and then write each sentence that you dictate.
a) My hair turned blue.   b) On Tuesdays we go to town.   c) The statue looks smart.

3. Letter hunt: Ask students to scan through the text carefully and underline all the 'ue' letters. Then they should read back through the text, this time reading for accuracy and meaning. Ask a question to check understanding, for example: *Why did Sue argue with Mum?*

4. Now it's your turn: Ask students to write three of their own short sentences using at least one word per sentence that contains today's focus code.

5. Challenge: Ask students to think about the challenge question. Draw attention to the knowledge that the ue spelling of the /y+oo/ and /oo/ sounds is used in the middle and at the end of words.

Student Workbook 1 Lesson 41 er as in herb and sister   **he, to**

Warm up: Ask students to turn to the chart on page 6 and point to the letters that match the sound you say. Call out a selection of sounds from Chart 3 at a brisk pace, allowing just enough time for learners to scan and point to the letters each time.

Introduction: Explain to students that the letters er are code for the sounds /er/ as in herb and /uh/ as in sister. The sound /er/ can also be speled: -er, ir, ur, ear, (w) or. The sound /uh/ can also be spelled: -er, -our, -re, -ar, -or. Today we are focusing on the er spelling of the /er/ and /uh/ sounds.

1. Word reading: Ask students to read each word carefully and tick to self-assess each word read. The words are *hermit, stern, thermal, jumper, temper* and *slipper*. Discuss any new or unusual word meanings.

2. Dictation time: Ask students to listen carefully and then write each sentence that you dictate.
a) I am going to perform in the show.   b) Perhaps it will rain.   c) I help to serve dinner.

3. Letter hunt: Ask students to scan through the text carefully and underline all the 'er' letters. Then they should read back through the text, this time reading for accuracy and meaning. Ask a question to check understanding, for example: *What hit the kerb?*

4. Now it's your turn: Ask students to write three of their own short sentences using at least one word per sentence that contains today's focus code.

5. Challenge: Ask students to think about the challenge question. Draw attention to the knowledge that the er spelling of the /er/ and /uh/ sounds isn't used at the beginning of words.

Student Workbook 1 Lesson 42 ar as in artist   **to, they**

Warm up: Ask students to turn to the chart on page 6 and practise saying the sounds with a partner. One says the sounds in the shaded boxes, the other says the sounds in the white boxes, then swap.

Introduction: Explain to students that the letters ar are code for the sound /ar/ as in artist. There are other ways to spell the /ar/ sound: ar, a, al. Today we are focusing on the ar spelling of the /ar/ sound.

1. Word reading: Ask students to read each word carefully and tick to self-assess each word read. The words are *ajar, dark, armpit, charm, shark, alarm* and *garden*. Discuss any new or unusual word meanings.

2. Dictation time: Ask students to listen carefully and then write each sentence that you dictate.
a) I am an artist.   b) It was still dark when we started.   c) I looked on the chart to order the parts.

3. Letter hunt: Ask students to scan through the text carefully and underline all the 'ar' letters. Then they should read back through the text, this time reading for accuracy and meaning. Ask a question to check understanding, for example: *Who went to the market?*

4. Now it's your turn: Ask students to write three of their own short sentences using at least one word per sentence that contains today's focus code.

5. Challenge: Ask students to think about the challenge question. Draw attention to the knowledge that the ar spelling of the /ar/ sound is used at the beginning, in the middle and at the end of words.

Warm up: Ask students to turn to the chart on page 6 and point to the letters that match the sound you say. Call out a selection of sounds from Chart 3 at a brisk pace, allowing just enough time for learners to scan and point to the letters each time.

Introduction: Explain to students that the letters ce are code for the sound /s/ as in palace. There are other ways to spell the /s/ sound: s, -ss, -ce, -se, c(e, i, y), sc, -st- or ps. Today we are focusing on the ce spelling of the /s/ sound.

1. Word reading: Ask students to read each word carefully and tick to self-assess each word read. The words are *fence, dance, prince, voice, force, advanced* and *choice*. Discuss any new or unusual word meanings.

2. Dictation time: Ask students to listen carefully and then write each sentence that you dictate.
a) Alice dreams of romance.   b) The bird sat on the fence.   c) I can force the lid off.

3. Letter hunt: Ask students to scan through the text carefully and underline all the 'ce' letters. Then they should read back through the text, this time reading for accuracy and meaning. Ask a question to check understanding, for example: *Who was Horace?*

4. Now it's your turn: Ask students to write three of their own short sentences using at least one word per sentence that contains today's focus code.

5. Challenge: Ask students to think about the challenge question. Draw attention to the knowledge that the ce spelling of the /s/ sound is used at the end of words. If students suggest words spelled with ce elsewhere, help them to say the word clearly and slowly to hear that the e is also pronounced in those words, for example, celery, century, celebrate. In those cases, c alone rather than ce is code for /s/.

Warm up: Ask students to turn to the chart on page 6 and practise saying the sounds with a partner. One says the sounds in the shaded boxes, the other says the sounds in the white boxes, then swap.

Introduction: Explain to students that the letters ge are code for the sound /j/ as in cabbage. There are other ways to spell the /j/ sound: j, -dge, -ge, g(e, i, y). Today we are focusing on the ge spelling of the /j/ sound.

1. Word reading: Ask students to read each word carefully and tick to self-assess each word read. The words are *forge, hinge, damage, package, savage* and *manage*. Discuss any new or unusual word meanings.

2. Dictation time: Ask students to listen carefully and then write each sentence that you dictate.
a) A large barge sits on the canal.   b) I managed to lift the package.   c) My luggage is damaged.

3. Letter hunt: Ask students to scan through the text carefully and underline all the 'ge' letters. Then they should read back through the text, this time reading for accuracy and meaning. Ask a question to check understanding, for example: *How did Marge do damage?*

4. Now it's your turn: Ask students to write three of their own short sentences using at least one word per sentence that contains today's focus code.

5. Challenge: Ask students to think about the challenge question. Draw attention to the knowledge that the ge spelling of the /j/ sound is used at the end of words. If students suggest words spelled with ge elsewhere, help them to say the word clearly and slowly to hear that the e is also pronounced in those words, for example, gem, gentle, general. In those cases, g alone rather than ge is code for /j/.

Student Workbook 1 Lesson 45 se as in house	he, no

Warm up: Ask students to turn to the chart on page 6 and point to the letters that match the sound you say. Call out a selection of sounds from Chart 3 at a brisk pace, allowing just enough time for learners to scan and point to the letters each time.

Introduction: Explain to students that the letters se are code for the sound /s/ as in house. There are other ways to spell the /s/ sound: s, -ss, -ce, -se, c(e, i, y), sc, -st- or ps. Today we are focusing on the se spelling of the /s/ sound.

1. Word reading: Ask students to read each word carefully and tick to self-assess each word read. The words are *sense, tense, horse, mouse, expense* and *immense*. Discuss any new or unusual word meanings.

2. Dictation time: Ask students to listen carefully and then write each sentence that you dictate.
a) We saw a horse and cart.   b) The mouse popped out of his hole.   c) The storm was intense.

3. Letter hunt: Ask students to scan through the text carefully and underline all the 'se' letters. Then they should read back through the text, this time reading for accuracy and meaning. Ask a question to check understanding, for example: *Who had a temper?*

4. Now it's your turn: Ask students to write three of their own short sentences using at least one word per sentence that contains today's focus code.

5. Challenge: Ask students to think about the challenge question. Draw attention to the knowledge that the se spelling of the /s/ sound is used at the end of words. If students suggest words spelled with se elsewhere, help them to say the word clearly and slowly to hear that the e is also pronounced in those words, for example, settle, send, separate. In those cases, s alone rather than se is code for /s/.

Student Workbook 1 Lesson 46 Word level assessment

Word reading: Listen to students read each of the words.

trowel	accrue	dishes	trance	android
grouse	chatty	above	dread	smooth
maximum	hooves	twinge	saddle	greasy
tease	sorted	undone	cloudy	perform
frizz	sparkle	squeal	gloat	balloon
cries	freed	whelk	oyster	brains

Word dictation: Dictate these words for students to write.

1. scowl	11. exit	21. jazzy
2. statue	12. groove	22. twinkle
3. crash	13. image	23. squashes
4. palace	14. middle	24. boast
5. avoid	15. mean	25. bell
6. mouse	16. please	26. tries
7. silly	17. form	27. greed
8. dove	18. some	28. wheels
9. instead	19. louder	29. joy
10. moon	20. termly	30. train

☐ **Lesson 1**: c(e, I, y)

☐ **Lesson 2**: g(e, I, y)

☐ **Lesson 3**: i-e as in time

☐ **Lesson 4**: e-e as in theme

☐ **Lesson 5**: o-e as in rope

☐ **Lesson 6**: a-e as in cake

☐ **Lesson 7**: u-e as in cute and flute

☐ **Lesson 8**: air as in hair

☐ **Lesson 9**: are as in hare

☐ **Lesson 10**: ear as in bear

☐ **Lesson 11**: ere as in where

☐ **Lesson 12**: eer as in deer

☐ **Lesson 13**: ear as in ears

☐ **Lesson 14**: ere as in adhere

☐ **Lesson 15**: ier as in cashier

☐ **Lesson 16**: ir as in birthday

☐ **Lesson 17**: ur as in nurse

☐ **Lesson 18**: ear as in earth

☐ **Lesson 19**: (w)or as in world

☐ **Lesson 20**: our as in humour

☐ **Lesson 21**: re as in theatre

☐ **Lesson 22**: le as in kettle

☐ **Lesson 23**: il as in pencil

☐ **Lesson 24**: al as in hospital

☐ **Lesson 25**: el as in camel

☐ **Lesson 26**: aw as in dawn

☐ **Lesson 27**: au as in sauce

☐ **Lesson 28**: al as in chalk

☐ **Lesson 29**: oar as in oars

☐ **Lesson 30**: oor as in door

☐ **Lesson 31**: ore as in snore

☐ **Lesson 32**: our as in four

☐ **Lesson 33**: tch as in patch

☐ **Lesson 34**: dge as in fridge

☐ **Lesson 35**: x as in exam

☐ **Lesson 36**: kn as in knot

☐ **Lesson 37**: wr as in write

☐ **Lesson 38**: mb as in thumb

☐ **Lesson 39**: sc as in scissors

☐ **Lesson 40**: gu as in guitar

☐ **Lesson 41**: bu as in building

☐ **Lesson 42**: ch as in chameleon

☐ **Lesson 43**: rh as in rhino

☐ **Lesson 44**: ch as in chef

☐ **Lesson 45**: ti as in station

☐ **Lesson 46**: ci as in magician

☐ **Lesson 47**: word assessment

☐ **Lesson 48**: text assessment

Student Workbook 2 Lesson 1 c (e, i, y)

Warm up: Ask students to turn to the chart on page 4 and practise saying the sounds with a partner. One says the sounds in the shaded boxes, the other says the sounds in the white boxes, then swap.

Introduction: Explain to students that the letter c is code for the sound /s/ when it is followed by an e, i or y. There are other ways to spell the sound /s/: s, ss, ce, se, c (e, i, y), sc, st or ps. Today we are focusing on the c (e, i, y) spelling of the /s/ sound.

1. Word reading: Ask students to read each word carefully and tick to self-assess each word read. The words are *city, cents, central, cellar, citrus, cygnet* and *cinema*. Discuss any new or unusual word meanings.

2. Dictation time: Ask students to listen carefully and then write each sentence that you dictate.
a) Can we celebrate my birthday?   b) December is the best month.   c) I am afraid of the cellar.

3. Letter hunt: Ask students to scan through the text carefully and underline all the c letters that are code for the /s/ sound. Then they should read the text, this time reading for accuracy and meaning. Ask a question to check understanding, for example: *How did Cinderella feel held back?*

4. Now it's your turn: Ask students to write three of their own short sentences using at least one word per sentence that contains today's focus code.

5. Challenge: Ask students to think about the challenge question. Draw attention to the knowledge that the c spelling of the /s/ sound is used at the beginning and in the middle of words.

Student Workbook 2 Lesson 2 g (e, i, y)

Warm up: Ask students to turn to the chart on page 4 and point to the letters that match the sound you say. Call out a selection of sounds from Chart 1 at a brisk pace, allowing just enough time for learners to scan and point to the letters each time.

Introduction: Explain to students that the letter g is code for the sound /j/ when it is followed by an e, i or y. There are other ways to spell the sound /j/: j, dge, ge or g (e, i, y). Today we are focusing on the g (e, i, y) spelling of the /j/ sound.

1. Word reading: Ask students to read each word carefully and tick to self-assess each word read. The words are *gem, germ, gentle, giraffe, ginger, energy* and *allergy*. Discuss any new or unusual word meanings.

2. Dictation time: Ask students to listen carefully and then write each sentence that you dictate.
a) Gillian is a gymnast.   b) The giant apologised.   c) The genius made the seeds germinate.

3. Letter hunt: Ask students to scan through the text carefully and underline all the g letters that are code for the /j/ sound. Then they should read the text, this time reading for accuracy and meaning. Ask a question to check understanding, for example: *Why did Gilly have lots of energy?*

4. Now it's your turn: Ask students to write three of their own short sentences using at least one word per sentence that contains today's focus code.

5. Challenge: Ask students to think about the challenge question. Draw attention to the knowledge that the g spelling of the /j/ sound is used at the beginning and in the middle of words.

Student Workbook 2 Lesson 3 i-e as in time.

Warm up: Ask students to turn to the chart on page 4 and practise saying the sounds with a partner. One says the sounds in the shaded boxes, the other says the sounds in the white boxes, then swap.

Introduction: Explain to students that the letters i-e are code for the sound /igh/ as in time. There are other ways to spell the /igh/ sound: -igh, -ie, i, -y, i-e or ei. Today we are focusing on the i-e spelling of the /igh/ sound.

1. Word reading: Ask students to read each word carefully and tick to self-assess each word read. The words are *time, hide, like, mice, inside, mime, swiped* and *slime*. Discuss any new or unusual word meanings.

2. Dictation time: Ask students to listen carefully and then write each sentence that you dictate.
a) Mike likes to hide outside.   b) We spotted a crime at the slide.   c) I like lime in my drink.

3. Letter hunt: Ask students to scan through the text carefully and underline all the i-e letters that are code for the /igh/ sound. Then they should read the text, this time reading for accuracy and meaning. Ask a question to check understanding, for example: *Why do you think Mike needed to get rid of mice?*

4. Now it's your turn: Ask students to write three of their own short sentences using at least one word per sentence that contains today's focus code.

5. Challenge: Ask students to think about the challenge question. Draw attention to the knowledge that the grapheme (letters) i-e do not always represent an /igh/ sound. In the word 'like', i-e is code for /igh/. In the word 'give', the sounds are g-i-ve. The word 'live' is a homophone so can be pronounced with a long or short vowel sound depending on the meaning of the word in context.

Student Workbook 2 Lesson 4 e-e as in theme

Warm up: Ask students to turn to the chart on page 4 and point to the letters that match the sound you say. Call out a selection of sounds from Chart 1 at a brisk pace, allowing just enough time for learners to scan and point to the letters each time.

Introduction: Explain to students that the letters e-e are code for the sound /ee/ as in theme. There are other ways to spell the /ee/ sound: ee, e, e-e, -ey, -ie, ei, ea or -y. Today we are focusing on the e-e spelling of the /ee/ sound.

1. Word reading: Ask students to read each word carefully and tick to self-assess each word read. The words are *stampede, even, theme, swede, extreme* and *compete*. Discuss any new or unusual word meanings.

2. Dictation time: Ask students to listen carefully and then write each sentence that you dictate.
a) Pete wrote a book with a fun theme.   b) Eve is a trapeze artist.   c) Steve likes extreme sports.

3. Letter hunt: Ask students to scan through the text carefully and underline all the e-e letters that are code for the /ee/ sound. Then they should read the text, this time reading for accuracy and meaning. Ask a question to check understanding, for example: *What was the main part of the play?*

4. Now it's your turn: Ask students to write three of their own short sentences using at least one word per sentence that contains today's focus code.

5. Challenge: Ask students to think about the challenge question. Encourage and support them to use dictionaries to define the words. *Concede*: admit or agree that something is true, surrender or yield.

Precede: come before something, go in front or ahead. *Obsolete*: no longer produced or used, out of date.

Student Workbook 2 Lesson 5 o-e as in rope

Warm up: Ask students to turn to the chart on page 4 and practise saying the sounds with a partner. One says the sounds in the shaded boxes, the other says the sounds in the white boxes, then swap.

Introduction: Explain to students that the letters o-e are code for the sound /oa/ as in rope. There are other ways to spell the /oa/ sound: oa, o, -oe, o-e, ow, -ough and -eau. Today we are focusing on the o-e spelling of the /oa/ sound.

1. Word reading: Ask students to read each word carefully and tick to self-assess each word read. The words are *stone, code, throne, alone, slope, globe* and *smoke*. Discuss any new or unusual word meanings.

2. Dictation time: Ask students to listen carefully and then write each sentence that you dictate.
a) We need a long rope.   b) The dog munched on a bone.   c) The king sits on his throne.

3. Letter hunt: Ask students to scan through the text carefully and underline all the o-e letters that are code for the /oa/ sound. Then they should read the text, this time reading for accuracy and meaning. Ask a question to check understanding, for example: *What did Hope do?*

4. Now it's your turn: Ask students to write three of their own short sentences using at least one word per sentence that contains today's focus code.

5. Challenge: Ask students to think about the challenge question. Encourage and support them to use dictionaries to define the words. *Scope*: the extent, the opportunity or to look carefully. *Abode*: place of residence. *Probe*: a small blunt-ended instrument; explore or examine.

Student Workbook 2 Lesson 6 a-e as in cake

Warm up: Ask students to turn to the chart on page 4 and point to the letters that match the sound you say. Call out a selection of sounds from Chart 1 at a brisk pace, allowing just enough time for learners to scan and point to the letters each time.

Introduction: Explain to students that the letters a-e are code for the sound /ai/ as in cake. There are other ways to spell the /ai/ sound: ai, ay, -ae, a-e, -ey, eigh, -ea and -aigh. Today we are focusing on the a-e spelling of the /ai/ sound.

1. Word reading: Ask students to read each word carefully and tick to self-assess each word read. The words are *daze, pace, blame, graceful, shame, place* and *make*. Discuss any new or unusual word meanings.

2. Dictation time: Ask students to listen carefully and then write each sentence that you dictate.
a) The singer wanted fame.   b) We played the computer game.   c) The goat is lame.

3. Letter hunt: Ask students to scan through the text carefully and underline all the a-e letters that are code for the /ai/ sound. Then they should read the text, this time reading for accuracy and meaning. Ask a question to check understanding, for example: *Where was the race held?*

4. Now it's your turn: Ask students to write three of their own short sentences using at least one word per sentence that contains today's focus code.

5. Challenge: Ask students to think about the challenge question. Encourage and support them to use dictionaries to define the words. *Fate*: destined to happen. *Instigate*: to set in motion. *Infiltrate*: to enter or become part of something.

Student Workbook 2 Lesson 7 u-e as in cute and flute

Warm up: Ask students to turn to the chart on page 4 and practise saying the sounds with a partner. One says the sounds in the shaded boxes, the other says the sounds in the white boxes, then swap.

Introduction: Explain to students that the letters u-e are code for the sounds /y+oo/ as in cute and /oo/ as in flute. There are also other ways to spell these sounds. They can both look like this: -ue, u-e or ew. Today we are focusing on the u-e spelling of the /y+oo/ and /oo/ sounds.

1. Word reading: Ask students to read each word carefully and tick to self-assess each word read. The words are *cute, rule, tube, salute, refuse, duke, amused* and *tune*. Discuss any new or unusual word meanings.

2. Dictation time: Ask students to listen carefully and then write each sentence that you dictate.
a) My birthday is in June.   b) The box is a cube.   c) The duke was a brute.

3. Letter hunt: Ask students to scan through the text carefully and underline all the u-e letters that are code for the /y+oo/ and /oo/ sounds. Then they should read the text, this time reading for accuracy and meaning. Ask a question to check understanding, for example: *How did Duke feel about Robert's flute playing?*

4. Now it's your turn: Ask students to write three of their own short sentences using at least one word per sentence that contains today's focus code.

5. Challenge: Ask students to think about the challenge question. For most accents…The /y+oo/ words are: cute, tube, refuse, duke, amused, tune. The /oo/ words are: rule, salute, flute, dude. Note – regional accent and dialect may affect which words contain each pronunciation in which case discuss and acknowledge.

Student Workbook 2 Lesson 8 air as in hair

Warm up: Ask students to turn to the chart on page 4 and point to the letters that match the sound you say. Call out a selection of sounds from Chart 1 at a brisk pace, allowing just enough time for learners to scan and point to the letters each time.

Introduction: Explain to students that the letters air are code for the sound /air/ as in hair. There are other ways to spell the /air/ sound: air, -are, -ear or -ere. Today we are focusing on the air spelling of the /air/ sound.

1. Word reading: Ask students to read each word carefully and tick to self-assess each word read. The words are *pair, chair, dairy, despair, repair, stairs, fair* and *hair*. Discuss any new or unusual word meanings.

2. Dictation time: Ask students to listen carefully and then write each sentence that you dictate.
a) The tooth fairy collects teeth.   b) I ate a cream éclair.   c) I have a new pair of boots.

3. Letter hunt: Ask students to scan through the text carefully and underline all the air letters that are code for the /air/ sound. Then they should read the text, this time reading for accuracy and meaning. Ask a question to check understanding, for example: *Why did the farmer despair?*

4. Now it's your turn: Ask students to write three of their own short sentences using at least one word per sentence that contains today's focus code.

5. Challenge: Ask students to think about the challenge question. Draw attention to the knowledge that the words *stair* and *stare* sound the same but have different meanings and are spelled in different ways. Likewise, *hair* and *hare* sound the same but have different meanings and are spelled differently. These words can be described as homophones. Discuss the word meanings.

Student Workbook 2 Lesson 9 are as in hare

Warm up: Ask students to turn to the chart on page 4 and practise saying the sounds with a partner. One says the sounds in the shaded boxes, the other says the sounds in the white boxes, then swap.

Introduction: Explain to students that the letters are are code for the sound /air/ as in hare. There are other ways to spell the /air/ sound: air, -are, -ear or -ere. Today we are focusing on the are spelling of the /air/ sound.

1. Word reading: Ask students to read each word carefully and tick to self-assess each word read. The words are *square, dared, compare, barely, spare* and *share*. Discuss any new or unusual word meanings.

2. Dictation time: Ask students to listen carefully and then write each sentence that you dictate.
a) The hare ran across the road.   b) I squinted to avoid the glare.   cI paid my taxi fare.

3. Letter hunt: Ask students to scan through the text carefully and underline all the are letters that are code for the /air/ sound. Then they should read the text, this time reading for accuracy and meaning. Ask a question to check understanding, for example: *Why were the gang scared?*

4. Now it's your turn: Ask students to write three of their own short sentences using at least one word per sentence that contains today's focus code.

5. Challenge: Ask students to think about the challenge question. Encourage and support them to use dictionaries to define the words. *Fanfare*: a short ceremonial tune, or media attention. *Declare*: announce something. *Wares*: pottery or articles for sale.

Student Workbook 2 Lesson 10 ear as in bear

Warm up: Ask students to turn to the chart on page 4 and point to the letters that match the sound you say. Call out a selection of sounds from Chart 1 at a brisk pace, allowing just enough time for learners to scan and point to the letters each time.

Introduction: Explain to students that the letters ear are code for the sound /air/ as in bear. There are other ways to spell the /air/ sound: air, -are, -ear or -ere. Today we are focusing on the ear spelling of the /air/ sound.

1. Word reading: Ask students to read each word carefully and tick to self-assess each word read. The words are *swear, tear, wear, bearer, unbearable* and *tearing*. Discuss any new or unusual word meanings.

2. Dictation time: Ask students to listen carefully and then write each sentence that you dictate.
a) The pear was ripe.   b) I saw a brown bear.   c) You must not swear in class.

3. Letter hunt: Ask students to scan through the text carefully and underline all the ear letters that are code for the /air/ sound. Then they should read the text, this time reading for accuracy and meaning. Ask a question to check understanding, for example: *Why was Will embarrassed?*

4. Now it's your turn: Ask students to write three of their own short sentences using at least one word per sentence that contains today's focus code.

5. Challenge: Ask students to think about the challenge question. Draw attention to the knowledge that the words *tear* and *tear* look the same but have different meanings and are pronounced in different ways. *Bear* and *bare* sound the same but have different meanings and are spelled differently. *Tear* and *tear* are homonyms. *Bear* and *bare* are homophones.

Student Workbook 2 Lesson 11 ere as in where

Warm up: Ask students to turn to the chart on page 4 and practise saying the sounds with a partner. One says the sounds in the shaded boxes, the other says the sounds in the white boxes, then swap.

Introduction: Explain to students that the letters ere are code for the sound /air/ as in where. There are other ways to spell the /air/ sound: air, -are, -ear or -ere. Today we are focusing on the ere spelling of the /air/ sound.

1. Word reading: Ask students to read each word carefully and tick to self-assess each word read. The words are *there, where, whereabouts, wherever* and *somewhere*. Discuss any new or unusual word meanings.

2. Dictation time: Ask students to listen carefully and then write each sentence that you dictate.
a) There are three pens on the desk.   b) Where is Sam?   c) Everywhere is shut.

3. Letter hunt: Ask students to scan through the text carefully and underline all the ere letters that are code for the /air/ sound. Then they should read the text, this time reading for accuracy and meaning. Ask a question to check understanding, for example: *Who was stuck in traffic?*

4. Now it's your turn: Ask students to write three of their own short sentences using at least one word per sentence that contains today's focus code.

5. Challenge: Ask students to think about the challenge question. Draw attention to the knowledge that the words *where, ware* and *wear* all sound the same but have different meanings and are spelled differently. They are homophones. Discuss the word meanings.

Student Workbook 2 Lesson 12 eer as in deer

Warm up: Ask students to turn to the chart on page 4 and point to the letters that match the sound you say. Call out a selection of sounds from Chart 1 at a brisk pace, allowing just enough time for learners to scan and point to the letters each time.

Introduction: Explain to students that the letters eer are code for the sound /eer/ as in deer. There are other ways to spell the /eer/ sound: eer, ear, -ere or -ier. Today we are focusing on the eer spelling of the /eer/ sound.

1. Word reading: Ask students to read each word carefully and tick to self-assess each word read. The words are *deer, sneer, volunteer, cheer, career, sheer* and *steer*. Discuss any new or unusual word meanings.

2. Dictation time: Ask students to listen carefully and then write each sentence that you dictate.
a) Peer out of the window.   b) We cheered when we won.   c) Jayden jeered at the kids.

3. Letter hunt: Ask students to scan through the text carefully and underline all the eer letters that are code for the /eer/ sound. Then they should read the text, this time reading for accuracy and meaning. Ask a question to check understanding, for example: *Why did Edward sneer?*

4. Now it's your turn: Ask students to write three of their own short sentences using at least one word per sentence that contains today's focus code.

5. Challenge: Ask students to think about the challenge question. Draw attention to the knowledge that the words *deer* and *dear* sound the same but have different meanings and are spelled differently. They are homophones. Discuss the word meanings.

Student Workbook 2 Lesson 13 ear as in ears

Warm up: Ask students to turn to the chart on page 4 and practise saying the sounds with a partner. One says the sounds in the shaded boxes, the other says the sounds in the white boxes, then swap.

Introduction: Explain to students that the letters ear are code for the sound /eer/ as in ears. There are other ways to spell the /eer/ sound: eer, ear, -ere or -ier. Today we are focusing on the ear spelling of the /eer/ sound.

1. Word reading: Ask students to read each word carefully and tick to self-assess each word read. The words are *hear, fear, appear, shears, nearly, tearful* and *year*. Discuss any new or unusual word meanings.

2. Dictation time: Ask students to listen carefully and then write each sentence that you dictate.
a) I went to see my dear old nan.   b) I will sit near Dan.   c) The cat disappeared.

3. Letter hunt: Ask students to scan through the text carefully and underline all the ear letters that are code for the /eer/ sound. Then they should read the text, this time reading for accuracy and meaning. Ask a question to check understanding, for example: *What happened to Emily?*

4. Now it's your turn: Ask students to write three of their own short sentences using at least one word per sentence that contains today's focus code.

5. Challenge: Ask students to think about the challenge question. Draw attention to the knowledge that the words *here* and *hear* sound the same but have different meanings and are spelled differently. They are homophones. Discuss the word meanings.

Student Workbook 2 Lesson 14 ere as in adhere

Warm up: Ask students to turn to the chart on page 4 and point to the letters that match the sound you say. Call out a selection of sounds from Chart 1 at a brisk pace, allowing just enough time for learners to scan and point to the letters each time.

Introduction: Explain to students that the letters ere are code for the sound /eer/ as in adhere. There are other ways to spell the /eer/ sound: eer, ear, -ere or -ier. Today we are focusing on the ere spelling of the /eer/ sound.

1. Word reading: Ask students to read each word carefully and tick to self-assess each word read. The words are *here, mere, interfere, persevere, sincerely* and *merely*. Discuss any new or unusual word meanings.

2. Dictation time: Ask students to listen carefully and then write each sentence that you dictate.
a) The letter was sincere.   b) I will sit here.   c) The punishment was severe.

3. Letter hunt: Ask students to scan through the text carefully and underline all the ere letters that are code for the /eer/ sound. Then they should read the text, this time reading for accuracy and meaning. Ask a question to check understanding, for example: *Can you describe Ravi?*

4. Now it's your turn: Ask students to write three of their own short sentences using at least one word per sentence that contains today's focus code.

5. Challenge: Ask students to think about the challenge question. Draw attention to the knowledge that the words *here* and *there* contain the same ere spelling pattern but in each word, it represents a different sound. In *here* the sound is /eer/ and in *there* the sound is /air/.

Student Workbook 2 Lesson 15 ier as in cashier

Warm up: Ask students to turn to the chart on page 4 and practise saying the sounds with a partner. One says the sounds in the shaded boxes, the other says the sounds in the white boxes, then swap.

Introduction: Explain to students that the letters ier are code for the sound /eer/ as in cashier. There are other ways to spell the /eer/ sound: eer, ear, -ere or -ier. Today we are focusing on the ier spelling of the /eer/ sound.

1. Word reading: Ask students to read each word carefully and tick to self-assess each word read. The words are *tier, pier, fierce, cashier, piercing, frontier* and *skier*. Discuss any new or unusual word meanings.

2. Dictation time: Ask students to listen carefully and then write each sentence that you dictate.
a) The cake had three tiers.   b) We sat on the pier.   c) My dad is a strong skier.

3. Letter hunt: Ask students to scan through the text carefully and underline all the ier letters that are code for the /eer/ sound. Then they should read the text, this time reading for accuracy and meaning. Ask a question to check understanding, for example: *Why were Tanya and Sally at the pier?*

4. Now it's your turn: Ask students to write three of their own short sentences using at least one word per sentence that contains today's focus code.

5. Challenge: Ask students to think about the challenge question. Encourage and support them to use dictionaries to define the words. *Cavalier*: a breed of dog; lack of concern. *Chandelier*: a large, decorative hanging light.

Student Workbook 2 Lesson 16 ir as in birthday

Warm up: Ask students to turn to the chart on page 4 and point to the letters that match the sound you say. Call out a selection of sounds from Chart 1 at a brisk pace, allowing just enough time for learners to scan and point to the letters each time.

Introduction: Explain to students that the letters ir are code for the sound /er/ as in birthday. There are other ways to spell the /er/ sound: er, ir, ur, ear and (w)or. The w inside brackets shows that the letters or can represent an er sound only following a w like in worm or world. The w isn't part of the sound, it acts as an alert for the pronunciation of the or as /er/. Today we are focusing on the ir spelling of the /er/ sound.

1. Word reading: Ask students to read each word carefully and tick to self-assess each word read. The words are *dirt, first, third, birthday, squirted, thirsty* and *stir*. Discuss any new or unusual word meanings.

2. Dictation time: Ask students to listen carefully and then write each sentence that you dictate.

a) The birds sing in the morning.   b) My shirt is pink.   c) There are fir trees in the park.

3. Letter hunt: Ask students to scan through the text carefully and underline all the ir letters that are code for the /er/ sound. Then they should read the text, this time reading for accuracy and meaning. Ask a question to check understanding, for example: *How many friends was Miss Dirst meeting?*

4. Now it's your turn: Ask students to write three of their own short sentences using at least one word per sentence that contains today's focus code.

5. Challenge: Ask students to think about the challenge question. Draw attention to the knowledge that the words bird, curl, earth and world all contain the /er/ sound in the middle, but that in each case the sound is spelled differently (ir, ur, ear, or)

Student Workbook 2 Lesson 17 ur as in nurse

Warm up: Ask students to turn to the chart on page 4 and practise saying the sounds with a partner. One says the sounds in the shaded boxes, the other says the sounds in the white boxes, then swap.

Introduction: Explain to students that the letters ur are code for the sound /er/ as in nurse. There are other ways to spell the /er/ sound: er, ir, ur, ear and (w)or. Today we are focusing on the ur spelling of the /er/ sound.

1. Word reading: Ask students to read each word carefully and tick to self-assess each word read. The words are *surf, turn, burglar, murder, purse, murmur* and *burnt*. Discuss any new or unusual word meanings.

2. Dictation time: Ask students to listen carefully and then write each sentence that you dictate.
a) We had burgers for lunch.   b) The cat lurked in the dark.   c) The farmer churned the butter.

3. Letter hunt: Ask students to scan through the text carefully and underline all the ur letters that are code for the /er/ sound. Then they should read the text, this time reading for accuracy and meaning. Ask a question to check understanding, for example: *How did the burglar get into the surgery?*

4. Now it's your turn: Ask students to write three of their own short sentences using at least one word per sentence that contains today's focus code.

5. Challenge: Ask students to think about the challenge question. Encourage and support them to use dictionaries to define the words. *Spurned*: rejected. *Unfurl*: become spread out from a rolled or folded position. *Murky*: dark, gloomy.

Student Workbook 2 Lesson 18 ear as earth

Warm up: Ask students to turn to the chart on page 4 and point to the letters that match the sound you say. Call out a selection of sounds from Chart 1 at a brisk pace, allowing just enough time for learners to scan and point to the letters each time.

Introduction: Explain to students that the letters ear are code for the sound /er/ as in earth. There are other ways to spell the /er/ sound: er, ir, ur, ear and (w)or. Today we are focusing on the ear spelling of the /er/ sound.

1. Word reading: Ask students to read each word carefully and tick to self-assess each word read. The words are *earn, earth, early, pearls, search, rehearsal* and *heard*. Discuss any new or unusual word meanings.

2. Dictation time: Ask students to listen carefully and then write each sentence that you dictate.

a) I searched for my sock.   b) I got home early.   c) There was a pearl in the oyster.

3. Letter hunt: Ask students to scan through the text carefully and underline all the ear letters that are code for the /er/ sound. Then they should read the text, this time reading for accuracy and meaning. Ask a question to check understanding, for example: *What did Pearl like to learn about?*

4. Now it's your turn: Ask students to write three of their own short sentences using at least one word per sentence that contains today's focus code.

5. Challenge: Ask students to think about the challenge question. Draw attention to the knowledge that the words hear and heard have the same root meaning and are spelled in a similar way but the pronunciation of the letters ear changes from an /eer/ sound in hear to and /er/ sound in heard.

Student Workbook 2 Lesson 19 (w)or as in world

Warm up: Ask students to turn to the chart on page 4 and practise saying the sounds with a partner. One says the sounds in the shaded boxes, the other says the sounds in the white boxes, then swap.

Introduction: Explain to students that the letters or are code for the sound /er/ when they come after a w, as in world. There are other ways to spell the /er/ sound: er, ir, ur, ear and (w)or. Today we are focusing on the or spelling of the /er/ sound.

1. Word reading: Ask students to read each word carefully and tick to self-assess each word read. The words are *worm, work, words, worst, worth, worthy* and *world*. Discuss any new or unusual word meanings.

2. Dictation time: Ask students to listen carefully and then write each sentence that you dictate.
a) I saw worms in the garden.   b) Working hard is worth the effort.   c) I travelled across the world.

3. Letter hunt: Ask students to scan through the text carefully and underline all the or letters that are code for the /er/ sound. Then they should read the text, this time reading for accuracy and meaning. Ask a question to check understanding, for example: *What is the difference between William and Wendy?*

4. Now it's your turn: Ask students to write three of their own short sentences using at least one word per sentence that contains today's focus code.

5. Challenge: Ask students to think about the challenge question. Draw attention to the knowledge that the or spelling of the /er/ sound always comes after the letter w and is positioned at the beginning of words.

Student Workbook 2 Lesson 20 our as in humour

Warm up: Ask students to turn to the chart on page 4 and point to the letters that match the sound you say. Call out a selection of sounds from Chart 1 at a brisk pace, allowing just enough time for learners to scan and point to the letters each time.

Introduction: Explain to students that the letters our are code for the sound schwa /er/ (uh) as in humour. There are other ways to spell the schwa /er/ sound: -er, -our, -re, ar and or. Today we are focusing on the our spelling of the schwa /er/ sound. 'Schwa' means unstressed syllable – when we speak we tend to replace many vowel syllables with an 'uh' type sound.

1. Word reading: Ask students to read each word carefully and tick to self-assess each word read. The words are *colour, favour, rumour, honour, glamour* and *flavour*. Discuss any new or unusual word meanings.

2. Dictation time: Ask students to listen carefully and then write each sentence that you dictate.
a) I heard a rumour.   b) I need to ask for a favour.   c) Red is the best colour.

3. Letter hunt: Ask students to scan through the text carefully and underline all the our letters that are code for the schwa /er/ sound. Then they should read the text, this time reading for accuracy and meaning. Ask a question to check understanding, for example: *What favour did Clare ask?*

4. Now it's your turn: Ask students to write three of their own short sentences using at least one word per sentence that contains today's focus code.

5. Challenge: Ask students to think about the challenge question. Draw attention to the knowledge that the word glamorous has the suffix -ous added to the end and the spelling of the schwa /er/ has changed from our to or.

Student Workbook 2 Lesson 21 re as in theatre

Warm up: Ask students to turn to the chart on page 4 and practise saying the sounds with a partner. One says the sounds in the shaded boxes, the other says the sounds in the white boxes, then swap.

Introduction: Explain to students that the letters re are code for the sound schwa /er/ (uh) as in theatre. There are other ways to spell the schwa /er/ sound: -er, -our, -re, ar and or. Today we are focusing on the re spelling of the schwa /er/ sound.

1. Word reading: Ask students to read each word carefully and tick to self-assess each word read. The words are *centre, metre, litre, ogre, fibre, millimetre* and *acre*. Discuss any new or unusual word meanings.

2. Dictation time: Ask students to listen carefully and then write each sentence that you dictate.
a) We went to the theatre.   b) My garden is an acre.   c) I drank a litre of milk.

3. Letter hunt: Ask students to scan through the text carefully and underline all the re letters that are code for the schwa /er/ sound. Then they should read the text, this time reading for accuracy and meaning. Ask a question to check understanding, for example: *What lesson was Dev in?*

4. Now it's your turn: Ask students to write three of their own short sentences using at least one word per sentence that contains today's focus code.

5. Challenge: Ask students to think about the challenge question. Encourage and support them to use dictionaries to define the words. *Timbre*: the tone of a musical sound. *Mediocre*: average, not very good. *Acre*: a unit of land equal to 4,840 square yards.

Student Workbook 2 Lesson 22 le as in kettle

Warm up: Ask students to turn to the chart on page 4 and point to the letters that match the sound you say. Call out a selection of sounds from Chart 1 at a brisk pace, allowing just enough time for learners to scan and point to the letters each time.

Introduction: Explain to students that the letters le are code for the sound /ul/ as in kettle. There are other ways to spell the /ul/ sound: -le, -il, -al and -el. Today we are focusing on the le spelling of the /ul/ sound.

1. Word reading: Ask students to read each word carefully and tick to self-assess each word read. The words are *niggles, sparkles, tackle, trickle, hackles* and *bottle*. Discuss any new or unusual word meanings.

2. Dictation time: Ask students to listen carefully and then write each sentence that you dictate.
a) I play the fiddle.   b) The horse got a new saddle.   c) I put pickle in my cheese roll.

3. Letter hunt: Ask students to scan through the text carefully and underline all the le letters that are code for the /ul/ sound. Then they should read the text, this time reading for accuracy and meaning. Ask a question to check understanding, for example: *Why was Mickey miserable?*

4. Now it's your turn: Ask students to write three of their own short sentences using at least one word per sentence that contains today's focus code.

5. Challenge: Ask students to think about the challenge question. Draw attention to the knowledge that many events over a long period of time have left our modern spellings in a pickle. English was formed over hundreds of years and was influenced by the native languages of people who came to settle in England such as the French and Romans. In the 15th century, when the first printers began making the first books in England, there was no uniform way to spell words so lots of inconsistencies were included.

Student Workbook 2 Lesson 23 il as in pencil

Warm up: Ask students to turn to the chart on page 4 and practise saying the sounds with a partner. One says the sounds in the shaded boxes, the other says the sounds in the white boxes, then swap.

Introduction: Explain to students that the letters il are code for the sound /ul/ as in pencil. There are other ways to spell the /ul/ sound: -le, -il, -al and -el. Today we are focusing on the il spelling of the /ul/ sound.

1. Word reading: Ask students to read each word carefully and tick to self-assess each word read. The words are *pupil, utensils, weevil, anvil, lentils, tonsils* and *April*. Discuss any new or unusual word meanings.

2. Dictation time: Ask students to listen carefully and then write each sentence that you dictate.
a) My birthday is in April.   b) I need to sharpen my pencil.   c) I used a stencil.

3. Letter hunt: Ask students to scan through the text carefully and underline all the il letters that are code for the /ul/ sound. Then they should read the text, this time reading for accuracy and meaning. Ask a question to check understanding, for example: *What was the flavour of the soup?*

4. Now it's your turn: Ask students to write three of their own short sentences using at least one word per sentence that contains today's focus code.

5. Challenge: Ask students to think about the challenge question. Encourage and support them to use dictionaries to define the words. *Vigil*: a period of keeping awake when you would normally sleep. *Basil*: a plant used as a herb in cooking. *Civil*: relating to citizens, polite.

Student Workbook 2 Lesson 24 as in hospital

Warm up: Ask students to turn to the chart on page 4 and point to the letters that match the sound you say. Call out a selection of sounds from Chart 1 at a brisk pace, allowing just enough time for learners to scan and point to the letters each time.

Introduction: Explain to students that the letters al are code for the sound /ul/ as in hospital. There are other ways to spell the /ul/ sound: -le, -il, -al and -el. Today we are focusing on the al spelling of the /ul/ sound.

1. Word reading: Ask students to read each word carefully and tick to self-assess each word read. The words are *manual, decimal, animal, several, hospital* and *signal*. Discuss any new or unusual word meanings.

2. Dictation time: Ask students to listen carefully and then write each sentence that you dictate.
a) We went to the capital.   b) I painted oval shapes.   c) We cheered at the final bell.

3. Letter hunt: Ask students to scan through the text carefully and underline all the al letters that are code for the /ul/ sound. Then they should read the text, this time reading for accuracy and meaning. Ask a question to check understanding, for example: *What is a virtual animal?*

4. Now it's your turn: Ask students to write three of their own short sentences using at least one word per sentence that contains today's focus code.

5. Challenge: Ask students to think about the challenge question. Encourage and support them to use dictionaries to define the words. *Virtual*: almost; not physically existing but made by software to appear so. *Capital*: the city or town that functions as the seat of government; wealth; upper-case letters; a serious offence. *Final*: at the end.

Student Workbook 2 Lesson 25 el as in camel

Warm up: Ask students to turn to the chart on page 4 and practise saying the sounds with a partner. One says the sounds in the shaded boxes, the other says the sounds in the white boxes, then swap.

Introduction: Explain to students that the letters el are code for the sound /ul/ as in camel. There are other ways to spell the /ul/ sound: -le, -il, -al and -el. Today we are focusing on the el spelling of the /ul/ sound.

1. Word reading: Ask students to read each word carefully and tick to self-assess each word read. The words are *panel, towel, travel, jewel, kennels, parcel* and *label*. Discuss any new or unusual word meanings.

2. Dictation time: Ask students to listen carefully and then write each sentence that you dictate.
a) The wooden panel was cracked.   b) My bath towel is soft.   c) The postman gave me a parcel.

3. Letter hunt: Ask students to scan through the text carefully and underline all the el letters that are code for the /ul/ sound. Then they should read the text, this time reading for accuracy and meaning. Ask a question to check understanding, for example: *What did Mr Marvel have for his wife?*

4. Now it's your turn: Ask students to write three of their own short sentences using at least one word per sentence that contains today's focus code.

5. Challenge: Ask students to think about the challenge question. Draw attention to the knowledge that el spelling of the /ul/ sound is positioned at the end of words. Notice though the addition of another l in travelling/travelled when suffixes are added; and notice the spelling of jewellery in comparison with the American spelling jewelry.

Student Workbook 2 Lesson 26 aw as in dawn

Warm up: Ask students to turn to the chart on page 4 and point to the letters that match the sound you say. Call out a selection of sounds from Chart 1 at a brisk pace, allowing just enough time for learners to scan and point to the letters each time.

Introduction: Explain to students that the letters aw are code for the sound /or/ as in dawn. There are other ways to spell the /or/ sound: or, ore, oar, -oor, -our, (w)ar, aw, au, -al, -augh and ough. Today we are focusing on the aw spelling of the /or/ sound.

1. Word reading: Ask students to read each word carefully and tick to self-assess each word read. The words are hawthorn, drawers, hawk, claws, squawk and paws. Discuss any new or unusual word meanings.

2. Dictation time: Ask students to listen carefully and then write each sentence that you dictate.
a) I like to draw portraits.   b) We got some metal straws.   c) I woke up at dawn.

3. Letter hunt: Ask students to scan through the text carefully and underline all the aw letters that are code for the /or/ sound. Then they should read the text, this time reading for accuracy and meaning. Ask a question to check understanding, for example: *How does the speaker protect their strawberries from the birds?*

4. Now it's your turn: Ask students to write three of their own short sentences using at least one word per sentence that contains today's focus code.

5. Challenge: Ask students to think about the challenge question. Encourage and support them to use dictionaries to define the words. *Flaw*: an imperfection. *Thaw*: defrost, become friendlier. *Dawning*: beginning.

Student Workbook 2 Lesson 27 au as in sauce

Warm up: Ask students to turn to the chart on page 4 and practise saying the sounds with a partner. One says the sounds in the shaded boxes, the other says the sounds in the white boxes, then swap.

Introduction: Explain to students that the letters au are code for the sound /or/ as in sauce. There are other ways to spell the /or/ sound: or, ore, oar, -oor, -our, (w)ar, aw, au, -al, -augh and ough. Today we are focusing on the au spelling of the /or/ sound.

1. Word reading: Ask students to read each word carefully and tick to self-assess each word read. The words are *applause, astronaut, audience, author* and *saucer*. Discuss any new or unusual word meanings.

2. Dictation time: Ask students to listen carefully and then write each sentence that you dictate.
a) My birthday is in August.   b) My sister is looking gaunt.   c) We think the house is haunted.

3. Letter hunt: Ask students to scan through the text carefully and underline all the au letters that are code for the /or/ sound. Then they should read the text, this time reading for accuracy and meaning. Ask a question to check understanding, for example: *Who was Paul Brown?*

4. Now it's your turn: Ask students to write three of their own short sentences using at least one word per sentence that contains today's focus code.

5. Challenge: Ask students to think about the challenge question. Encourage and support them to use dictionaries to define the words. *Haul*: pull or drag; a quantity of stolen goods. *Haunches*: buttocks and thigh. *Launch*: set in motion.

Student Workbook 2 Lesson 28 al as in chalk

Warm up: Ask students to turn to the chart on page 4 and point to the letters that match the sound you say. Call out a selection of sounds from Chart 1 at a brisk pace, allowing just enough time for learners to scan and point to the letters each time.

Introduction: Explain to students that the letters al are code for the sound /or/ as in chalk. There are other ways to spell the /or/ sound: or, ore, oar, -oor, -our, (w)ar, aw, au, -al, -augh and ough. Today we are focusing on the al spelling of the /or/ sound.

1. Word reading: Ask students to read each word carefully and tick to self-assess each word read. The words are *walk, stalk, small, call, stall, ball, talking* and *tallest*. Discuss any new or unusual word meanings.

2. Dictation time: Ask students to listen carefully and then write each sentence that you dictate.
a) The cat prowled along the garden wall.   b) I kicked the ball into the net.   c) We ran a cake stall.

3. Letter hunt: Ask students to scan through the text carefully and underline all the al letters that are code for the /or/ sound. Then they should read the text, this time reading for accuracy and meaning. Ask a question to check understanding, for example: *What does Mr Chalk say?*

4. Now it's your turn: Ask students to write three of their own short sentences using at least one word per sentence that contains today's focus code.

5. Challenge: Ask students to think about the challenge question. Draw attention to the knowledge that the letters 'al' in the words *also, almost* and *always* sound like /or/+/l/ - you can hear the 'l'. Try saying the words in comparison with words from the lesson. In the lesson words with /or/+/l/ contain a double l. The first letter l is part of the grapheme 'al' (representing the /or/ sound) and the second letter l.

Student Workbook 2 Lesson 29 oar as in oars

Warm up: Ask students to turn to the chart on page 4 and practise saying the sounds with a partner. One says the sounds in the shaded boxes, the other says the sounds in the white boxes, then swap.

Introduction: Explain to students that the letters oar are code for the sound /or/ as in oars. There are other ways to spell the /or/ sound: or, ore, oar, -oor, -our, (w)ar, aw, au, -al, -augh and ough. Today we are focusing on the oar spelling of the /or/ sound.

1. Word reading: Ask students to read each word carefully and tick to self-assess each word read. The words are *aboard, roar, hoard, keyboard, soar, oars* and *boar*. Discuss any new or unusual word meanings.

2. Dictation time: Ask students to listen carefully and then write each sentence that you dictate.
a) We played board games.   b) The birds soared above the rooftops.   c) My nan is a hoarder.

3. Letter hunt: Ask students to scan through the text carefully and underline all the oar letters that are code for the /or/ sound. Then they should read the text, this time reading for accuracy and meaning. Ask a question to check understanding, for example: *Who found some gold?*

4. Now it's your turn: Ask students to write three of their own short sentences using at least one word per sentence that contains today's focus code.

5. Challenge: Ask students to think about the challenge question. Draw attention to the knowledge that the words *hoarse* and *horse* sound the same but have different meanings and are spelled differently. They are homophones. Discuss the word meanings.

Student Workbook 2 Lesson 30 as in door

Warm up: Ask students to turn to the chart on page 4 and point to the letters that match the sound you say. Call out a selection of sounds from Chart 1 at a brisk pace, allowing just enough time for learners to scan and point to the letters each time.

Introduction: Explain to students that the letters oor are code for the sound /or/ as in door. There are other ways to spell the /or/ sound: or, ore, oar, -oor, -our, (w)ar, aw, au, -al, -augh and ough. Today we are focusing on the oor spelling of the /or/ sound.

1. Word reading: Ask students to read each word carefully and tick to self-assess each word read. The words are *door, floor, poorly, flooring, indoors* and *spoor*. Discuss any new or unusual word meanings.

2. Dictation time: Ask students to listen carefully and then write each sentence that you dictate.
a) I have been indoors all day.   b) Jake slammed the door.   c) The hunter looked for a spoor.

3. Letter hunt: Ask students to scan through the text carefully and underline all the oor letters that are code for the /or/ sound. Then they should read the text, this time reading for accuracy and meaning. Ask a question to check understanding, for example: *Why did Lewis walk across the cold floor?*

4. Now it's your turn: Ask students to write three of their own short sentences using at least one word per sentence that contains today's focus code.

5. Challenge: Ask students to think about the challenge question. Draw attention to the knowledge that the words *moor* and *more* sound the same but have different meanings and are spelled differently. Likewise, the words *poor* and *pour* sound the same but have different meanings and are spelled differently. They are homophones. Discuss the word meanings.

Student Workbook 2 Lesson 31 ore as in snore

Warm up: Ask students to turn to the chart on page 5 and practise saying the sounds with a partner. One says the sounds in the shaded boxes, the other says the sounds in the white boxes, then swap.

Introduction: Explain to students that the letters ore are code for the sound /or/ as in snore. There are other ways to spell the /or/ sound: or, ore, oar, -oor, -our, (w)ar, aw, au, -al, -augh and ough. Today we are focusing on the ore spelling of the /or/ sound.

1. Word reading: Ask students to read each word carefully and tick to self-assess each word read. The words are *galore, core, sore, bored, sycamore, before* and *score*. Discuss any new or unusual word meanings.

2. Dictation time: Ask students to listen carefully and then write each sentence that you dictate.
a) More apples have grown on the tree.   b) Turn the light off before you go.   c) On Saturday I do my chores.

3. Letter hunt: Ask students to scan through the text carefully and underline all the ore letters that are code for the /or/ sound. Then they should read the text, this time reading for accuracy and meaning. Ask a question to check understanding, for example: *Where was the swing?*

4. Now it's your turn: Ask students to write three of their own short sentences using at least one word per sentence that contains today's focus code.

5. Challenge: Ask students to think about the challenge question. Encourage and support them to use dictionaries to define the words. *Omnivore*: an animal that eats both plants and meat. *Herbivore*: an animal that eats plants (and not meat).

Student Workbook 2 Lesson 32 our as in four

Warm up: Ask students to turn to the chart on page 5 and point to the letters that match the sound you say. Call out a selection of sounds from Chart 2 at a brisk pace, allowing just enough time for learners to scan and point to the letters each time.

Introduction: Explain to students that the letters our are code for the sound /or/ as in four. There are other ways to spell the /or/ sound: or, ore, oar, -oor, -our, (w)ar, aw, au, -al, -augh and ough. Today we are focusing on the our spelling of the /or/ sound.

1. Word reading: Ask students to read each word carefully and tick to self-assess each word read. The words are *your, four, pour, court, fourth, mourn* and *course*. Discuss any new or unusual word meanings.

2. Dictation time: Ask students to listen carefully and then write each sentence that you dictate.
a) We mourned the loss of my grandpa.   b) You have dropped your pen.   c) The trial was held at the youth court.

3. Letter hunt: Ask students to scan through the text carefully and underline all the our letters that are code for the /or/ sound. Then they should read the text, this time reading for accuracy and meaning. Ask a question to check understanding, for example: *How long did it rain for?*

4. Now it's your turn: Ask students to write three of their own short sentences using at least one word per sentence that contains today's focus code.

5. Challenge: Ask students to think about the challenge question. Draw attention to the knowledge that the words *four* and *for* sound the same but have different meanings and are spelled differently. Likewise, the words *court* and *caught* sound the same but have different meanings and are spelled differently. They are homophones. Discuss the word meanings.

Student Workbook 2 Lesson 33 tch as in patch

Warm up: Ask students to turn to the chart on page 5 and practise saying the sounds with a partner. One says the sounds in the shaded boxes, the other says the sounds in the white boxes, then swap.

Introduction: Explain to students that the letters tch are code for the sound /ch/ as in patch. There are other ways to spell the /ch/ sound: ch or tch. Today we are focusing on the tch spelling of the /ch/ sound.

1. Word reading: Ask students to read each word carefully and tick to self-assess each word read. The words are *itch, hatch, batch, clutch, ditches, mismatch* and *pitch*. Discuss any new or unusual word meanings.

2. Dictation time: Ask students to listen carefully and then write each sentence that you dictate.
a) The van crashed into a ditch. b) We pitched our idea to the boss.   c) The chicks hatched from the eggs.

3. Letter hunt: Ask students to scan through the text carefully and underline all the tch letters that are code for the /ch/ sound. Then they should read the text, this time reading for accuracy and meaning. Ask a question to check understanding, for example: *Why did the speaker have to wait to eat the rolls?*

4. Now it's your turn: Ask students to write three of their own short sentences using at least one word per sentence that contains today's focus code.

5. Challenge: Ask students to think about the challenge question. Encourage and support them to use dictionaries to define the words. *Stretcher*: a framework of two poles with a long piece of canvas slung between them, used for carrying sick, injured or dead people. *Ditched*: give up, discard. *Latches*: a door or gate fastening.

Student Workbook 2 Lesson 34 dge as in fridge

Warm up: Ask students to turn to the charts on pages 4 and 5 and point to the letters that match the sound you say. Call out a selection of sounds at a brisk pace, allowing just enough time for learners to scan and point to the letters each time.

Introduction: Explain to students that the letters dge are code for the sound /j/ as in fridge. There are other ways to spell the /j/ sound: j, -dge, -ge and g (e, i, y). Today we are focusing on the dge spelling of the /j/ sound.

1. Word reading: Ask students to read each word carefully and tick to self-assess each word read. The words are *pledge, ridge, sledge, wedges, nudge, grudge* and *ledge*. Discuss any new or unusual word meanings.

2. Dictation time: Ask students to listen carefully and then write each sentence that you dictate.
a) I keep my eggs in the fridge.   b) The gardener trimmed the hedge.   c) We live near a famous bridge.

3. Letter hunt: Ask students to scan through the text carefully and underline all the dge letters that are code for the /j/ sound. Then they should read the text, this time reading for accuracy and meaning. Ask a question to check understanding, for example: *What did Hilda cook?*

4. Now it's your turn: Ask students to write three of their own short sentences using at least one word per sentence that contains today's focus code.

5. Challenge: Ask students to think about the challenge question. Encourage and support them to use dictionaries to define the words. *Sludge*: a dirty, muddy type of mixture. *Drudgery*: hard or dull work. *Dislodge*: move out of position.

Student Workbook 2 Lesson 35 x as in exam

Warm up: Ask students to turn to the charts on pages 4 and 5 and practise saying the sounds with a partner. One says the sounds in the shaded boxes, the other says the sounds in the white boxes, then swap.

Introduction: Explain to students that the letter x is code for the sound /g+z/ as in exam. The sound /g+z/ is actually two sounds /g/ and /z/ but it is useful for reading and spelling to learn as one sound unit. Today we are focusing on the x spelling of the /g+z/ sound.

1. Word reading: Ask students to read each word carefully and tick to self-assess each word read. The words are *exam, exact, exotic, example, exit* and *existence*. Discuss any new or unusual word meanings.

2. Dictation time: Ask students to listen carefully and then write each sentence that you dictate.
a) The exam took all afternoon.   b) We ran for the exit.   c) The textbook always contains an example.

3. Letter hunt: Ask students to scan through the text carefully and underline all the x letters that are code for the /g+z/ sound. Then they should read the text, this time reading for accuracy and meaning. Ask a question to check understanding, for example: *How does Helen feel about exams?*

4. Now it's your turn: Ask students to write three of their own short sentences using at least one word per sentence that contains today's focus code.

5. Challenge: Ask students to think about the challenge question. Encourage and support them to use dictionaries to define the words. *Exert*: make an effort. *Exhibit*: publicly display one's work; to show. *Exhaust*: make someone feel very tired; to use up resources.

Student Workbook 2 Lesson 36 kn as in knot

Warm up: Ask students to turn to the charts on pages 4 and 5 and point to the letters that match the sound you say. Call out a selection of sounds at a brisk pace, allowing just enough time for learners to scan and point to the letters each time.

Introduction: Explain to students that the letters kn are code for the sound /n/ as in knot. There are other ways to spell the /n/ sound: n, -nn, kn, gn or -ne. Today we are focusing on the kn spelling of the /n/ sound.

1. Word reading: Ask students to read each word carefully and tick to self-assess each word read. The words are *knee, kneel, knelt, knuckle, know, knit* and *knife*. Discuss any new or unusual word meanings.

2. Dictation time: Ask students to listen carefully and then write each sentence that you dictate.
a) There was a loud knock on the door.   b) The brave knight rode into town.   c) I cut the apple with a sharp knife.

3. Letter hunt: Ask students to scan through the text carefully and underline all the kn letters that are code for the /n/ sound. Then they should read the text, this time reading for accuracy and meaning. Ask a question to check understanding, for example: *How did the knight get hurt?*

4. Now it's your turn: Ask students to write three of their own short sentences using at least one word per sentence that contains today's focus code.

5. Challenge: Ask students to think about the challenge question. Draw attention to the knowledge that the kn spelling of the /n/ sound is used at the beginning of words.

Student Workbook 2 Lesson 37 wr as in write

Warm up: Ask students to turn to the charts on pages 4 and 5 and practise saying the sounds with a partner. One says the sounds in the shaded boxes, the other says the sounds in the white boxes, then swap.

Introduction: Explain to students that the letters wr are code for the sound /r/ as in write. There are other ways to spell the /r/ sound: r, -rr, wr or rh. Today we are focusing on the wr spelling of the /r/ sound.

1. Word reading: Ask students to read each word carefully and tick to self-assess each word read. The words are *wrap, wreck, wrist, wrinkle, wrapping* and *written*. Discuss any new or unusual word meanings.

2. Dictation time: Ask students to listen carefully and then write each sentence that you dictate.
a) I wrote a long letter to my nan.   b) The caterpillar wriggled on the leaf.   c) I hurt my wrist when I played basketball.

3. Letter hunt: Ask students to scan through the text carefully and underline all the wr letters that are code for the /r/ sound. Then they should read the text, this time reading for accuracy and meaning. Ask a question to check understanding, for example: *What did Tabitha see on her walk?*

4. Now it's your turn: Ask students to write three of their own short sentences using at least one word per sentence that contains today's focus code.

5. Challenge: Ask students to think about the challenge question. Draw attention to the knowledge that the wr spelling of the /r/ sound is used at the beginning of words.

Student Workbook 2 Lesson 38 mb as in thumb

Warm up: Ask students to turn to the charts on pages 4 and 5 and point to the letters that match the sound you say. Call out a selection of sounds at a brisk pace, allowing just enough time for learners to scan and point to the letters each time.

Introduction: Explain to students that the letters mb are code for the sound /m/ as in thumb. There are other ways to spell the /m/ sound: m, -mm, -me, -mb or mn. Today we are focusing on the mb spelling of the /m/ sound.

1. Word reading: Ask students to read each word carefully and tick to self-assess each word read. The words are *lamb, limb, numb, bomb, thumb, climb* and *plumber*. Discuss any new or unusual word meanings.

2. Dictation time: Ask students to listen carefully and then write each sentence that you dictate.
a) We saw the lambs being born.   b) I need a plumber to fix the taps.   c) The goat climbed the mountain.

3. Letter hunt: Ask students to scan through the text carefully and underline all the mb letters that are code for the /m/ sound. Then they should read the text, this time reading for accuracy and meaning. Ask a question to check understanding, for example: *What was Jayden's job?*

4. Now it's your turn: Ask students to write three of their own short sentences using at least one word per sentence that contains today's focus code.

5. Challenge: Ask students to think about the challenge question. Encourage and support them to use dictionaries to define the words. *Succumb*: give in. *Comb*: a strip of plastic, metal, or wood, with a row of narrow teeth used for untangling hair. *Tomb*: a large vault for burying the dead.

Student Workbook 2 Lesson 39 sc as in scissors

Warm up: Ask students to turn to the charts on pages 4 and 5 and practise saying the sounds with a partner. One says the sounds in the shaded boxes, the other says the sounds in the white boxes, then swap.

Introduction: Explain to students that the letters sc are code for the sound /s/ as in scissors. There are other ways to spell the /s/ sound: s, -ss, -ce, -se, c (e, i, y), sc, -st- or ps. Today we are focusing on the sc spelling of the /s/ sound.

1. Word reading: Ask students to read each word carefully and tick to self-assess each word read. The words are *scent, scissors, scene, scientist, scythe* and *science*. Discuss any new or unusual word meanings.

2. Dictation time: Ask students to listen carefully and then write each sentence that you dictate.
a) The scientist made an important discovery.   b) I have lost the scissors again.   c) I helped make scenery for the show.

3. Letter hunt: Ask students to scan through the text carefully and underline all the sc letters that are code for the /s/ sound. Then they should read the text, this time reading for accuracy and meaning. Ask a question to check understanding, for example: *How did the farmer trim the grass?*

4. Now it's your turn: Ask students to write three of their own short sentences using at least one word per sentence that contains today's focus code.

5. Challenge: Ask students to think about the challenge question. Draw attention to the knowledge that in this lesson the sc spelling of the /s/ sound is used at the beginning of words but there are words that contain this spelling in the middle such as: ascend and ascent.

Student Workbook 2 Lesson 40 gu as in guitar

Warm up: Ask students to turn to the charts on pages 4 and 5 and point to the letters that match the sound you say. Call out a selection of sounds at a brisk pace, allowing just enough time for learners to scan and point to the letters each time.

Introduction: Explain to students that the letters gu are code for the sound /g/ as in guitar. There are other ways to spell the /g/ sound: g, -gg, gu or -gue. Today we are focusing on the gu spelling of the /g/ sound.

1. Word reading: Ask students to read each word carefully and tick to self-assess each word read. The words are *guess, guest, guard, guilty, guide, disguise* and *guy*. Discuss any new or unusual word meanings.

2. Dictation time: Ask students to listen carefully and then write each sentence that you dictate.
a) We invited fifty guests to the party.   b) I enjoy playing the guitar.   c) My sister always looks guilty.

3. Letter hunt: Ask students to scan through the text carefully and underline all the gu letters that are code for the /g/ sound. Then they should read the text, this time reading for accuracy and meaning. Ask a question to check understanding, for example: *What did the guy carrying the guitar look like?*

4. Now it's your turn: Ask students to write three of their own short sentences using at least one word per sentence that contains today's focus code.

5. Challenge: Ask students to think about the challenge question. Draw attention to the knowledge that in this lesson the gu spelling of the /g/ sound is used at the beginning of words.

Student Workbook 2 Lesson 41 bu as in building

Warm up: Ask students to turn to the charts on pages 4 and 5 and practise saying the sounds with a partner. One says the sounds in the shaded boxes, the other says the sounds in the white boxes, then swap.

Introduction: Explain to students that the letters bu are code for the sound /b/ as in building. There are other ways to spell the /b/ sound: b, -bb or bu. Today we are focusing on the bu spelling of the /b/ sound.

1. Word reading: Ask students to read each word carefully and tick to self-assess each word read. The words are *buy, buyer, buoy, buoyant, builder* and *building*. Discuss any new or unusual word meanings.

2. Dictation time: Ask students to listen carefully and then write each sentence that you dictate.
a) We built a model of the fairground.   b) The boy clung to the buoy to help him float.   c) I am going to buy some sweets.

3. Letter hunt: Ask students to scan through the text carefully and underline all the bu letters that are code for the /b/ sound. Then they should read the text, this time reading for accuracy and meaning. Ask a question to check understanding, for example: *Why was the builder so buoyant?*

4. Now it's your turn: Ask students to write three of their own short sentences using at least one word per sentence that contains today's focus code.

5. Challenge: Ask students to think about the challenge question. Draw attention to the knowledge that the bu spelling of the /b/ sound is used at the beginning of words.

Student Workbook 2 Lesson 42 ch as in chameleon

Warm up: Ask students to turn to the charts on pages 4 and 5 and point to the letters that match the sound you say. Call out a selection of sounds at a brisk pace, allowing just enough time for learners to scan and point to the letters each time.

Introduction: Explain to students that the letters ch are code for the sound /k/ as in chameleon. There are other ways to spell the /k/ sound: k, c, -ck, ch, qu or que. Today we are focusing on the ch spelling of the /k/ sound.

1. Word reading: Ask students to read each word carefully and tick to self-assess each word read. The words are *school, chorus, chemist, character, chronic* and *cholera*. Discuss any new or unusual word meanings.

2. Dictation time: Ask students to listen carefully and then write each sentence that you dictate.
a) An arachnid is a spider.   b) I play the drums in an orchestra.   c) My mum is a mechanic.

3. Letter hunt: Ask students to scan through the text carefully and underline all the ch letters that are code for the /k/ sound. Then they should read the text, this time reading for accuracy and meaning. Ask a question to check understanding, for example: *What caused chaos?*

4. Now it's your turn: Ask students to write three of their own short sentences using at least one word per sentence that contains today's focus code.

5. Challenge: Ask students to think about the challenge question. Draw attention to the knowledge that the sounds represented by the letters ch are: /ch/ as in chair; /k/ as in school and /sh/ as in chef.

Student Workbook 2 Lesson 43 rh as in rhino

Warm up: Ask students to turn to the charts on pages 4 and 5 and practise saying the sounds with a partner. One says the sounds in the shaded boxes, the other says the sounds in the white boxes, then swap.

Introduction: Explain to students that the letters rh are code for the sound /r/ as in rhino. There are other ways to spell the /r/ sound: r, -rr, wr or rh. Today we are focusing on the rh spelling of the /r/ sound.

1. Word reading: Ask students to read each word carefully and tick to self-assess each word read. The words are *rhubarb, rhino, rhombus, rhymes, rhetoric* and *rhythm*. Discuss any new or unusual word meanings.

2. Dictation time: Ask students to listen carefully and then write each sentence that you dictate.
a) We saw rhinos on the safari tour.   b) I like to write poems that rhyme.   c) A rhombus is a shape.

3. Letter hunt: Ask students to scan through the text carefully and underline all the rh letters that are code for the /r/ sound. Then they should read the text, this time reading for accuracy and meaning. Ask a question to check understanding, for example: *Where did Ronnie dance?*

4. Now it's your turn: Ask students to write three of their own short sentences using at least one word per sentence that contains today's focus code.

5. Challenge: Ask students to think about the challenge question. Encourage and support them to use dictionaries to define the words. *Rhapsody*: a free instrumental composition in one extended movement. *Rhebok*: a small South African antelope. *Rhinestone*: an imitation diamond, used in cheap jewellery and to decorate clothes.

Student Workbook 2 Lesson 44 ch as in chef

Warm up: Ask students to turn to the charts on pages 4 and 5 and point to the letters that match the sound you say. Call out a selection of sounds at a brisk pace, allowing just enough time for learners to scan and point to the letters each time.

Introduction: Explain to students that the letters ch are code for the sound /sh/ as in chef. There are other ways to spell the /sh/ sound: sh, ch, -ti, -ci or -ssi. Today we are focusing on the ch spelling of the /sh/ sound.

1. Word reading: Ask students to read each word carefully and tick to self-assess each word read. The words are *chiffon, chute, chaperone, machine* and *charades*. Discuss any new or unusual word meanings.

2. Dictation time: Ask students to listen carefully and then write each sentence that you dictate.
a) We have a chandelier in our hallway.   b) The chef cooked a grand feast.   c) The new machine was broken.

3. Letter hunt: Ask students to scan through the text carefully and underline all the ch letters that are code for the /sh/ sound. Then they should read the text, this time reading for accuracy and meaning. Ask a question to check understanding, for example: *What do you think happened to the shirts?*

4. Now it's your turn: Ask students to write three of their own short sentences using at least one word per sentence that contains today's focus code.

5. Challenge: Ask students to think about the challenge question. Encourage and support them to use dictionaries to define the words. *Chivalry*: courteous behaviour. *Chassis*: the base frame of a car or carriage. *Chalet*: a wooden house with overhanging eaves, typically found in the Swiss alps.

Student Workbook 2 Lesson 45 ti as in station

Warm up: Ask students to turn to the charts on pages 4 and 5 and practise saying the sounds with a partner. One says the sounds in the shaded boxes, the other says the sounds in the white boxes, then swap.

Introduction: Explain to students that the letters ti are code for the sound /sh/ as in station. There are other ways to spell the /sh/ sound: sh, ch, -ti, -ci or -ssi. Today we are focusing on the ti spelling of the /sh/ sound.

1. Word reading: Ask students to read each word carefully and tick to self-assess each word read. The words are *nation, motion, station, patient, partial* and *essential*. Discuss any new or unusual word meanings.

2. Dictation time: Ask students to listen carefully and then write each sentence that you dictate.
a) I have designed a new invention.   b) I have a good imagination.   c) The soup was like a potion.

3. Letter hunt: Ask students to scan through the text carefully and underline all the ti letters that are code for the /sh/ sound. Then they should read the text, this time reading for accuracy and meaning. Ask a question to check understanding, for example: *What situation is urgent?*

4. Now it's your turn: Ask students to write three of their own short sentences using at least one word per sentence that contains today's focus code.

5. Challenge: Ask students to think about the challenge question. Draw attention to the knowledge that the ti spelling of the /sh/ sound is used in the middle of words.

Student Workbook 2 Lesson 46 ci as in magician

Warm up: Ask students to turn to the charts on pages 4 and 5 and point to the letters that match the sound you say. Call out a selection of sounds at a brisk pace, allowing just enough time for learners to scan and point to the letters each time.

Introduction: Explain to students that the letters ci are code for the sound /sh/ as in magician. There are other ways to spell the /sh/ sound: sh, ch, -ti, -ci or -ssi. Today we are focusing on the ci spelling of the /sh/ sound.

1. Word reading: Ask students to read each word carefully and tick to self-assess each word read. The words are *official, special, musician, ancient* and *artificial.* Discuss any new or unusual word meanings.

2. Dictation time: Ask students to listen carefully and then write each sentence that you dictate.
a) We planned a special dinner.   b) My sister has a job at the official offices.   c) My brother is a musician.

3. Letter hunt: Ask students to scan through the text carefully and underline all the ci letters that are code for the /sh/ sound. Then they should read the text, this time reading for accuracy and meaning. Ask a question to check understanding, for example: *Why was Patience's mother suspicious?*

4. Now it's your turn: Ask students to write three of their own short sentences using at least one word per sentence that contains today's focus code.

5. Challenge: Ask students to think about the challenge question. Draw attention to the knowledge that the ci spelling of the /sh/ sound is used in the middle of words.

Student Workbook 2 Lesson 47 Word level assessment

Word reading: Listen to students read each of the words.

cinema	vertical	nowhere	niggles	third
spurned	gentle	research	career	prawns
scraped	launch	crime	flannel	nearly
weevil	amused	litre	swede	chalk
sincere	board	flair	ignore	throne
flavour	cavalier	emotion	declare	worst

Word dictation: Dictate these words for students to write.

1. ginger	11. bottle	21. chemist
2. theme	12. decimal	22. machine
3. graceful	13. squawk	23. ancient
4. dairy	14. tallest	24. citrus
5. wearing	15. floor	25. inside
6. cheer	16. pour	26. globe
7. mere	17. nudge	27. refuse
8. birthday	18. knelt	28. compare
9. pearl	19. climb	29. wherever
10. colour	20. guest	30. year

Student Workbook 2 Lesson 48 Text level assessment

Text reading: Listen to students read the passage or ask them to read to a partner and self-assess their confidence in reading the passage.

It was the start of the autumn term and all the students pledged to try their best. Despite good intentions, things soon turned crazy. Susan had an allergic reaction to a science experiment. An ambulance had to be sent to take her to hospital. Students gathered around to watch the unfolding scene. Next a large number of staff came down with a terrible tickle in their throats. They blamed the onset of cold and damp weather which had been long overdue after a sweltering summer. The registers got muddled and teachers called students by the wrong surnames. By the third week of term everybody needed a holiday. Instead they had to start play rehearsals if they wanted to be ready by Christmas. At least the new school website was launched successfully so virtual guests could increase their knowledge of the school and its policies.

Text dictation: Dictate this passage for students to write.

Last year we moved to a new city. It is a big city with lots of gyms, theatres, hospitals, office buildings and a train station. There are lots of jobs in the city. You can be a nurse, a chef, a bank cashier or even a guitarist if you want to. I hope to be a writer when I am older. I will write about animals like chameleons and camels, rhinos and bears. I will put the kettle on, enjoy some cake and write about the world.

KS3 Phonics Student Workbook 3 Contents

Student Workbook 3 Lesson 1 ssi as in admission

Warm up: Ask students to turn to the chart on page 4 and point to the letters that match the sound you say. Call out a selection of sounds from Chart 1 at a brisk pace, allowing just enough time for learners to scan and point to the letters each time.

Introduction: Explain to students that there are several graphemes which represent the /sh/ sound: sh, ch, -ti, -ci and -ssi. Note that the end of every word in this lesson is spelt -ssion and this word chunk is pronounced "shun".

1. Word reading: Ask students to read each word carefully and tick to self-assess each word read. The words are *mission, admission, permission, passion, expression, discussion, compassion* and *possession*. Discuss any new or unusual word meanings.

2. Dictation time: Ask students to listen carefully and then write each sentence that you dictate.
a) The team started the mission.   b) We paid full price admission for the concert.   c) Most of the lesson was a discussion.

3. Letter hunt: Ask students to scan through the text carefully and underline all the ssi letters that are code for the /sh/ sound. Then they should read the text, this time reading for accuracy and meaning. Ask a question to check understanding, for example: *How did Sally know that the gatekeeper was a robot?*

4. Now it's your turn: Ask students to write three of their own short sentences using at least one word per sentence that contains today's focus code.

Student Workbook 3 Lesson 2 /zh/ as in treasure

Warm up: Ask students to turn to the chart on page 4 and practise saying the sounds with a partner. One says the sounds in the shaded boxes, the other says the sounds in the white boxes, then swap.

Introduction: Explain to students that the words in today's lesson have an unusual pronunciation which is denoted as /zh/. You could almost describe this sound as 'soft z'.

1. Word reading: Ask students to read each word carefully and tick to self-assess each word read. The words are *television, confusion, invasion, illusion, measure, treasure, casual, usual, delusion, courgette, azure* and *visual*. Discuss any new or unusual word meanings.

2. Dictation time: Ask students to listen carefully and then write each sentence that you dictate.
a) The test was full of division questions.   b) The performer created some amazing illusions.   c) We measured our ingredients carefully.

3. Letter hunt: Ask students to scan through the text carefully and underline all the letters that are code for the /zh/ sound. Then they should read the text, this time reading for accuracy and meaning. Ask a question to check understanding, for example: *Why did Crystal say that the survey was not accurate?*

4. Now it's your turn: Ask students to write three of their own short sentences using at least one word per sentence that contains today's focus code.

Student Workbook 3 Lesson 3 ou as in touch

Warm up: Ask students to turn to the chart on page 4 and point to the letters that match the sound you say. Call out a selection of sounds from Chart 1 at a brisk pace, allowing just enough time for learners to scan and point to the letters each time.

Introduction: Explain to students that the grapheme 'ou' is another way of representing the /u/ phoneme. It is most commonly used as part of the 'ous' suffix which forms adjectives such as 'famous'.

1. Word reading: Ask students to read each word carefully and tick to self-assess each word read. The words are *couple, cousin, flourish, famous, enormous, enough, troubles, double, rough, touch, serious* and *nourish*. Discuss any new or unusual word meanings.

2. Dictation time: Ask students to listen carefully and then write each sentence that you dictate.
a) My uncle has a large moustache.   b) We rode in a limousine to the prom.   c) The elephant painting was enormous.

3. Letter hunt: Ask students to scan through the text carefully and underline all the ou letters that are code for the /u/ sound. Then they should read the text, this time reading for accuracy and meaning. Ask a question to check understanding, for example: *How many people can fit in James' limousine?*

4. Now it's your turn: Ask students to write three of their own short sentences using at least one word per sentence that contains today's focus code.

Student Workbook 3 Lesson 4 ous as in precious

Warm up: Ask students to turn to the chart on page 4 and practise saying the sounds with a partner. One says the sounds in the shaded boxes, the other says the sounds in the white boxes, then swap.

Introduction: Explain to students that the suffix 'ous' commonly forms adjectives. The suffix 'ous' is made from two pieces of code: 'ou' as /u/ + 's' as /s/.

1. Word reading: Ask students to read each word carefully and tick to self-assess each word read. The words are *anonymous, porous, previous, rigorous, hideous, hilarious, dangerous, numerous, courteous, tedious* and *curious*. Discuss any new or unusual word meanings.

2. Dictation time: Ask students to listen carefully and then write each sentence that you dictate.
a) Sometimes I find reading tedious.   b) My bedroom is a hazardous place.   c) You should try not to feel envious of others.

3. Letter hunt: Ask students to scan through the text carefully and underline all the 'ous' suffixes. Then they should read the text, this time reading for accuracy and meaning. Ask a question to check understanding, for example: *How is Angela planning to avoid the salespeople?*

4. Now it's your turn: Ask students to write three of their own short sentences using at least one word per sentence that contains today's focus code.

Student Workbook 3 Lesson 5 ph as in photograph

Warm up: Ask students to turn to the chart on page 4 and point to the letters that match the sound you say. Call out a selection of sounds from Chart 1 at a brisk pace, allowing just enough time for learners to scan and point to the letters each time.

Introduction: Explain to students that the grapheme 'ph' is another way of representing the /f/ phoneme. The words 'photo' and 'phone' are shortened versions of 'photograph' and 'telephone'.

1. Word reading: Ask students to read each word carefully and tick to self-assess each word read. The words are *telegraph, orphan, photo, phase, phone, elephant, sphere, hemisphere, phrase, triumph, phobia* and *phantom*. Discuss any new or unusual word meanings.

2. Dictation time: Ask students to listen carefully and then write each sentence that you dictate.
a) I am learning to take better photographs.   b) My new puppy is an orphan.   c) I can't wait to watch 'Phantom of the Opera'.

3. Letter hunt: Ask students to scan through the text carefully and underline all the ph letters that are code for the /f/ sound. Then they should read the text, this time reading for accuracy and meaning. Ask a question to check understanding, for example: *Who is Phyllis?*

4. Now it's your turn: Ask students to write three of their own short sentences using at least one word per sentence that contains today's focus code.

Student Workbook 3 Lesson 6 gh as in laugh

Warm up: Ask students to turn to the chart on page 4 and practise saying the sounds with a partner. One says the sounds in the shaded boxes, the other says the sounds in the white boxes, then swap.

Introduction: Explain to students that the grapheme 'gh' is another way of representing the /f/ phoneme. In the word examples, the grapheme 'ou' is sometimes /u/ and sometimes /o/. The 'au' can be /a/ or /ar/.

1. Word reading: Ask students to read each word carefully and tick to self-assess each word read. The words are *rough, tough, tougher, enough, roughage, cough, coughing, trough, laugh, laughter* and *draughts*. Discuss any new or unusual word meanings.

2. Dictation time: Ask students to listen carefully and then write each sentence that you dictate.
a) I was coughing all night long.   b) That obstacle course was harder than I expected.   c) We laughed and laughed when the balloon popped.

3. Letter hunt: Ask students to scan through the text carefully and underline all the gh letters that are code for the /f/ sound. Then they should read the text, this time reading for accuracy and meaning. Ask a question to check understanding, for example: *Why did Mohammed say that his Grandmother was so tough?*

4. Now it's your turn: Ask students to write three of their own short sentences using at least one word per sentence that contains today's focus code.

Student Workbook 3 Lesson 7 gh as in ghost

Warm up: Ask students to turn to the chart on page 4 and point to the letters that match the sound you say. Call out a selection of sounds from Chart 1 at a brisk pace, allowing just enough time for learners to scan and point to the letters each time.

Introduction: Explain to students that the sound /g/ is represented by four graphemes: g, gg, gh and gue. The grapheme 'gh' is a rare grapheme although people are aware of it because of the words in this lesson.

1. Word reading: Ask students to read each word carefully and tick to self-assess each word read. The words are *ghost, ghettos, ghastly, ghoul, ghostwriter, gherkin, ghetto, ghost town, spaghetti* and *Ghana*. Discuss any new or unusual word meanings.

2. Dictation time: Ask students to listen carefully and then write each sentence that you dictate.
a) We cooked fresh spaghetti for lunch.   b) I always pick out the gherkins and leave them.   c) The streets were as empty as a ghost town.

3. Letter hunt: Ask students to scan through the text carefully and underline all the letters that are code for the /g/ sound. Then they should read the text, this time reading for accuracy and meaning. Ask a question to check understanding, for example: *What is Gavin's job?*

4. Now it's your turn: Ask students to write three of their own short sentences using at least one word per sentence that contains today's focus code.

Student Workbook 3 Lesson 8 (w)a as in watch

Warm up: Ask students to turn to the chart on page 4 and practise saying the sounds with a partner. One says the sounds in the shaded boxes, the other says the sounds in the white boxes, then swap.

Introduction: Explain to students that the where the letter 'w' precedes the letter 'a', the reader is alerted to the possibility that the 'a' might be pronounced as the /o/ phoneme.

1. Word reading: Ask students to read each word carefully and tick to self-assess each word read. The words are *want, wasp, wand, wash, waft, watch, waffle, wander, swan, swap, swamp, swallow, swat* and *swashbuckling*. Discuss any new or unusual word meanings.

2. Dictation time: Ask students to listen carefully and then write each sentence that you dictate.
a) We collected swatches of fabric for the project.   b) My watch can play music and track steps.
c) The swamp was full of alligators.

3. Letter hunt: Ask students to scan through the text carefully and underline all the wa letters that are code for the /wo/ sound. Then they should read the text, this time reading for accuracy and meaning. Ask a question to check understanding, for example: *What did Wanda think about the film?*

4. Now it's your turn: Ask students to write three of their own short sentences using at least one word per sentence that contains today's focus code.

Student Workbook 3 Lesson 9 (qu)a as in qualify

Warm up: Ask students to turn to the chart on page 4 and point to the letters that match the sound you say. Call out a selection of sounds from Chart 1 at a brisk pace, allowing just enough time for learners to scan and point to the letters each time.

Introduction: Explain to students that the where the grapheme 'qu' precedes the letter 'a', the reader is alerted to the possibility that the 'a' might be pronounced as the /o/ phoneme.

1. Word reading: Ask students to read each word carefully and tick to self-assess each word read. The words are *quarry, quarrel, quality, squat, squash, squabble, squatter, squalor, squander, squad, squadron, quadrangle* and *qualify*. Discuss any new or unusual word meanings.

2. Dictation time: Ask students to listen carefully and then write each sentence that you dictate.
a) I hope to get some good qualifications.   b) The animals had to go into quarantine.
c) Sometimes I squabble with my siblings.

3. Letter hunt: Ask students to scan through the text carefully and underline all the qua letters that are code for the /quo/ sound. Then they should read the text, this time reading for accuracy and meaning. Ask a question to check understanding, for example: *Who was building a memorial?*

4. Now it's your turn: Ask students to write three of their own short sentences using at least one word per sentence that contains today's focus code.

Student Workbook 3 Lesson 10 (w)ar as in wardrobe

Warm up: Ask students to turn to the chart on page 4 and practise saying the sounds with a partner. One says the sounds in the shaded boxes, the other says the sounds in the white boxes, then swap.

Introduction: Explain to students that the where the letter 'w' precedes the grapheme 'ar', the reader is alerted to the possibility that the 'ar' might be pronounced as the /or/ phoneme.

1. Word reading: Ask students to read each word carefully and tick to self-assess each word read. The words are *war, warm, warmth, warn, wart, ward, warden, warp, towards, warning, wartime* and *wardrobe*. Discuss any new or unusual word meanings.

2. Dictation time: Ask students to listen carefully and then write each sentence that you dictate.
a) We visited Grandpa on Darwin ward.   b) The afternoon sun warmed me up.   c) The warden came running towards us.

3. Letter hunt: Ask students to scan through the text carefully and underline all the war letters that are code for the /wor/ sound. Then they should read the text, this time reading for accuracy and meaning. Ask a question to check understanding, for example: *Why was Sasha's mother on the warpath?*

4. Now it's your turn: Ask students to write three of their own short sentences using at least one word per sentence that contains today's focus code.

Student Workbook 3 Lesson 11 gn as in gnome

Warm up: Ask students to turn to the chart on page 4 and point to the letters that match the sound you say. Call out a selection of sounds from Chart 1 at a brisk pace, allowing just enough time for learners to scan and point to the letters each time.

Introduction: Explain to students that the grapheme 'gn' is another way of representing the /n/ phoneme. In the example words, the grapheme 'ei' is pronounced /ai/.

1. Word reading: Ask students to read each word carefully and tick to self-assess each word read. The words are *gnat, gnaw, gnash, gnarled, gnome, sign, align, reign, feign, malign, design, campaign, designer* and *consignment*. Discuss any new or unusual word meanings.

2. Dictation time: Ask students to listen carefully and then write each sentence that you dictate.
a) If you hate your job you can resign.   b) Our garden gnome has gone missing.   c) I have designed my own t-shirt.

3. Letter hunt: Ask students to scan through the text carefully and underline all the gn letters that are code for the /n/ sound. Then they should read the text, this time reading for accuracy and meaning. Ask a question to check understanding, for example: *Is the gnome in the text friendly or not?*

4. Now it's your turn: Ask students to write three of their own short sentences using at least one word per sentence that contains today's focus code.

Student Workbook 3 Lesson 12 st as in castle

Warm up: Ask students to turn to the chart on page 4 and practise saying the sounds with a partner. One says the sounds in the shaded boxes, the other says the sounds in the white boxes, then swap.

Introduction: Explain to students that the grapheme 'st' is another way of representing the /s/ phoneme. It is usually used within the words.

1. Word reading: Ask students to read each word carefully and tick to self-assess each word read. The words are *hustle, bustle, whistling, rustle, trestle, jostle, wrestle, castle, thistle, gristle, nestle, listen, fasten* and *hasten*. Discuss any new or unusual word meanings.

2. Dictation time: Ask students to listen carefully and then write each sentence that you dictate.
a) The fastener on my bag is stuck.   b) It is hard to listen when there is background noise.   c) My garden is overgrown and full of thistles.

3. Letter hunt: Ask students to scan through the text carefully and underline all the st letters that are code for the /s/ sound. Then they should read the text, this time reading for accuracy and meaning. Ask a question to check understanding, for example: *What happens at the castle?*

4. Now it's your turn: Ask students to write three of their own short sentences using at least one word per sentence that contains today's focus code.

Student Workbook 3 Lesson 13 ey as in prey

Warm up: Ask students to turn to the chart on page 4 and point to the letters that match the sound you say. Call out a selection of sounds from Chart 1 at a brisk pace, allowing just enough time for learners to scan and point to the letters each time.

Introduction: Explain to students that the grapheme 'ey' is another way of representing the /ai/ phoneme. This grapheme is used rarely to represent the /ai/ sound but some words, like 'they' and 'grey' are common words.

1. Word reading: Ask students to read each word carefully and tick to self-assess each word read. The words are *they, grey, survey, prey, obey, disobey, surveyor, convey, conveyed, heyday, conveyance* and *whey*. Discuss any new or unusual word meanings.

2. Dictation time: Ask students to listen carefully and then write each sentence that you dictate.
a) I put my shopping on the conveyor belt.   b) The surveyor was at the building site by seven am.
c) The owl caught its prey.

3. Letter hunt: Ask students to scan through the text carefully and underline all the ey letters that are code for the /ai/ sound. Then they should read the text, this time reading for accuracy and meaning. Ask a question to check understanding, for example: *How did the surveyor cheer everyone up?*

4. Now it's your turn: Ask students to write three of their own short sentences using at least one word per sentence that contains today's focus code.

Student Workbook 3 Lesson 14 eigh as in eight

Warm up: Ask students to turn to the chart on page 4 and practise saying the sounds with a partner. One says the sounds in the shaded boxes, the other says the sounds in the white boxes, then swap.

Introduction: Explain to students that the grapheme 'eigh' is another way of representing the /ai/ phoneme. This grapheme is used rarely to represent the /ai/ sound but most of the example words are commonly used.

1. Word reading: Ask students to read each word carefully and tick to self-assess each word read. The words are *eight, weigh, eighty, sleigh, weight, outweigh, eightieth, neighbour, neighbourhood, neighbourly* and *lightweight*. Discuss any new or unusual word meanings.

2. Dictation time: Ask students to listen carefully and then write each sentence that you dictate.

a) We rode on a sleigh on holiday.   b) This parcel weighs too much to carry.   c) My nan is eighty years old.

3. Letter hunt: Ask students to scan through the text carefully and underline all the eigh letters that are code for the /ai/ sound. Then they should read the text, this time reading for accuracy and meaning. Ask a question to check understanding, for example: *What event was the neighbourhood discussing?*

4. Now it's your turn: Ask students to write three of their own short sentences using at least one word per sentence that contains today's focus code.

Student Workbook 3 Lesson 15 ea as in break

Warm up: Ask students to turn to the chart on page 4 and point to the letters that match the sound you say. Call out a selection of sounds from Chart 1 at a brisk pace, allowing just enough time for learners to scan and point to the letters each time.

Introduction: Explain to students that the grapheme 'ea' is another way of representing the /ai/ phoneme. This grapheme is used rarely to represent the /ai/ sound but most of the example words are commonly used.

1. Word reading: Ask students to read each word carefully and tick to self-assess each word read. The words are *break, great, steak, breakage, windbreaker, breakwater, greatness, greatly, breakaway* and *Great Britain*. Discuss any new or unusual word meanings.

2. Dictation time: Ask students to listen carefully and then write each sentence that you dictate.
a) I think you are great.   b) There was a break in at the school.   c) Any breakages must be paid for at the china shop.

3. Letter hunt: Ask students to scan through the text carefully and underline all the ea letters that are code for the /ai/ sound. Then they should read the text, this time reading for accuracy and meaning. Ask a question to check understanding, for example: *Who used to run a steakhouse?*

4. Now it's your turn: Ask students to write three of their own short sentences using at least one word per sentence that contains today's focus code.

Student Workbook 3 Lesson 16 aigh as in straight

Warm up: Ask students to turn to the chart on page 4 and practise saying the sounds with a partner. One says the sounds in the shaded boxes, the other says the sounds in the white boxes, then swap.

Introduction: Explain to students that the grapheme 'aigh' is another way of representing the /ai/ phoneme. This grapheme is used rarely to represent the /ai/ sound but most of the example words are commonly used.

1. Word reading: Ask students to read each word carefully and tick to self-assess each word read. The words are *straight, straighten, straightforward, straightjacket, straightaway, straightedge* and *straightening*. Discuss any new or unusual word meanings.

2. Dictation time: Ask students to listen carefully and then write each sentence that you dictate.
a) I never do things straightaway.   b) The burglar was thinking about going straight.   c) Lots of girls like to straighten their hair.

3. Letter hunt: Ask students to scan through the text carefully and underline all the aigh letters that are code for the /ai/ sound. Then they should read the text, this time reading for accuracy and meaning. Ask a question to check understanding, for example: *Are you a straightforward person?*

4. Now it's your turn: Ask students to write three of their own short sentences using at least one word per sentence that contains today's focus code.

Student Workbook 3 Lesson 17 ey as in monkey

Warm up: Ask students to turn to the chart on page 4 and point to the letters that match the sound you say. Call out a selection of sounds from Chart 1 at a brisk pace, allowing just enough time for learners to scan and point to the letters each time.

Introduction: Explain to students that the grapheme 'ey' is another way of representing the sound between the /i/ and /ee/ phonemes depending on accent. The grapheme 'ey' also represents /ee/ as in key.

1. Word reading: Ask students to read each word carefully and tick to self-assess each word read. The words are *donkey, monkey, money, storey, chutney, journey, honeysuckle, paisley, parsley, galley, hockey* and *pulley*. Discuss any new or unusual word meanings.

2. Dictation time: Ask students to listen carefully and then write each sentence that you dictate.
a) We went on a long car journey.   b) I was thinking about adopting a donkey.   c) My new job pays good money.

3. Letter hunt: Ask students to scan through the text carefully and underline all the ey letters that are code for the /i-ee/ sound. Then they should read the text, this time reading for accuracy and meaning. Ask a question to check understanding, for example: *What was Maloney looking for?*

4. Now it's your turn: Ask students to write three of their own short sentences using at least one word per sentence that contains today's focus code.

Student Workbook 3 Lesson 18 ie as in movie

Warm up: Ask students to turn to the chart on page 4 and practise saying the sounds with a partner. One says the sounds in the shaded boxes, the other says the sounds in the white boxes, then swap.

Introduction: Explain to students that the grapheme 'ie' is another way of representing the sound between the /i/ and /ee/ phonemes depending on accent. It is often used in people's first names, e.g. Alfie.

1. Word reading: Ask students to read each word carefully and tick to self-assess each word read. The words are *movie, pixie, budgie, freebie, pinkie, rookie, oldie, calorie, hankie, collie, genie, cookie, pixies* and *cookies*. Discuss any new or unusual word meanings.

2. Dictation time: Ask students to listen carefully and then write each sentence that you dictate.
a) We watch a movie every Saturday night.   b) My social media name is Pinkie Pixie.   c) We got a budgie called Genie.

3. Letter hunt: Ask students to scan through the text carefully and underline all the ie letters that are code for the /i-ee/ sound. Then they should read the text, this time reading for accuracy and meaning. Ask a question to check understanding, for example: *What was the name of the pet budgie?*

4. Now it's your turn: Ask students to write three of their own short sentences using at least one word per sentence that contains today's focus code.

Student Workbook 3 Lesson 19 y as in cymbals

Warm up: Ask students to turn to the chart on page 4 and point to the letters that match the sound you say. Call out a selection of sounds from Chart 1 at a brisk pace, allowing just enough time for learners to scan and point to the letters each time.

Introduction: Explain to students that the grapheme 'y' is another way of representing the /i/ phoneme in the example words. The letter 'y' has a close relationship with the letter 'I' and the phonemes /i/ and /igh/.

1. Word reading: Ask students to read each word carefully and tick to self-assess each word read. The words are *system, symbol, syrup, crystal, mystery, gym, rhythm, myth, gymnastics, cymbal* and *mysterious*. Discuss any new or unusual word meanings.

2. Dictation time: Ask students to listen carefully and then write each sentence that you dictate.
a) I like writing mystery stories.   b) Our new headteacher is very mysterious.   c) We made milkshakes with strawberry syrup.

3. Letter hunt: Ask students to scan through the text carefully and underline all the y letters that are code for the /i/ sound. Then they should read the text, this time reading for accuracy and meaning. Ask a question to check understanding, for example: *Who is this text about?*

4. Now it's your turn: Ask students to write three of their own short sentences using at least one word per sentence that contains today's focus code.

Student Workbook 3 Lesson 20 ie as in chief

Warm up: Ask students to turn to the chart on page 4 and practise saying the sounds with a partner. One says the sounds in the shaded boxes, the other says the sounds in the white boxes, then swap.

Introduction: Explain to students that the grapheme 'ie' is another way of representing the /ee/ phoneme.

1. Word reading: Ask students to read each word carefully and tick to self-assess each word read. The words are *thief, brief, chief, relief, niece, grief, priest, series, field, species, frieze, diesel, hygiene, fiend, retriever* and *believe*. Discuss any new or unusual word meanings.

2. Dictation time: Ask students to listen carefully and then write each sentence that you dictate.
a) We walked through the fields.   b) Washing your hands is just good hygiene.   c) I believe that the chief has retired.

3. Letter hunt: Ask students to scan through the text carefully and underline all the ie letters that are code for the /ee/ sound. Then they should read the text, this time reading for accuracy and meaning. Ask a question to check understanding, for example: *How was the thief caught?*

4. Now it's your turn: Ask students to write three of their own short sentences using at least one word per sentence that contains today's focus code.

Student Workbook 3 Lesson 21 ei as in eider duck

Warm up: Ask students to turn to the chart on page 4 and point to the letters that match the sound you say. Call out a selection of sounds from Chart 1 at a brisk pace, allowing just enough time for learners to scan and point to the letters each time.

Introduction: Explain to students that the grapheme 'ei' is a very rare way of representing the /igh/ phoneme. The words 'either' and 'neither' are very common although some people pronounce them with an /ee/ sound.

1. Word reading: Ask students to read each word carefully and tick to self-assess each word read. The words are *either, eider duck, eiderdown, neither, heist, seismic, seismograph, poltergeist, Fahrenheit, feisty* and *Poseidon*. Discuss any new or unusual word meanings.

2. Dictation time: Ask students to listen carefully and then write each sentence that you dictate.
a) My duvet is stuffed with eiderdown.   b) My pet cat is very feisty.   c) I have neither the energy nor the time to exercise.

3. Letter hunt: Ask students to scan through the text carefully and underline all the ei letters that are code for the /igh/ sound. Then they should read the text, this time reading for accuracy and meaning. Ask a question to check understanding, for example: *Where does Heidi live?*

4. Now it's your turn: Ask students to write three of their own short sentences using at least one word per sentence that contains today's focus code.

Student Workbook 3 Lesson 22 o as in son

Warm up: Ask students to turn to the chart on page 4 and practise saying the sounds with a partner. One says the sounds in the shaded boxes, the other says the sounds in the white boxes, then swap.

Introduction: Explain to students that there are several graphemes which represent the /u/ sound and 'o' is a less common grapheme for this sound, although sometimes the words are common.

1. Word reading: Ask students to read each word carefully and tick to self-assess each word read. The words are *son, ton, won, wonder, wonderful, front, sponge, tongue, among, money, come, becoming, pigeon, love* and *onion*. Discuss any new or unusual word meanings.

2. Dictation time: Ask students to listen carefully and then write each sentence that you dictate.
a) My brother looks like my mother.   b) I wonder where that pigeon comes from.   c) I love onion gravy.

3. Letter hunt: Ask students to scan through the text carefully and underline all the o letters that are code for the /u/ sound. Then they should read the text, this time reading for accuracy and meaning. Ask a question to check understanding, for example: *What is the speaker's mother good at?*

4. Now it's your turn: Ask students to write three of their own short sentences using at least one word per sentence that contains today's focus code.

Student Workbook 3 Lesson 23 ew as in crew

Warm up: Ask students to turn to the chart on page 4 and point to the letters that match the sound you say. Call out a selection of sounds from Chart 1 at a brisk pace, allowing just enough time for learners to scan and point to the letters each time.

Introduction: Explain to students that there are many graphemes which represent the long /oo/ sound, including 'ew'. The grapheme 'ew' can also represent /yoo/.

1. Word reading: Ask students to read each word carefully and tick to self-assess each word read. The words are *yew tree, chew, brew, drew, threw, screw, shrew, shrewd, jewellery, corkscrew, cashew nuts, sewage* and *strewn*. Discuss any new or unusual word meanings.

2. Dictation time: Ask students to listen carefully and then write each sentence that you dictate.
a) My clothes are strewn across my bedroom.   b) We saw a little shrew in the garden.   c) We threw the ball back and forth.

3. Letter hunt: Ask students to scan through the text carefully and underline all the ew letters that are code for the long /oo/ sound. Then they should read the text, this time reading for accuracy and meaning. Ask a question to check understanding, for example: *What happened to the yew tree?*

4. Now it's your turn: Ask students to write three of their own short sentences using at least one word per sentence that contains today's focus code.

Student Workbook 3 Lesson 24 ui as in fruit

Warm up: Ask students to turn to the chart on page 4 and practise saying the sounds with a partner. One says the sounds in the shaded boxes, the other says the sounds in the white boxes, then swap.

Introduction: Explain to students that there are many graphemes which represent the long /oo/ sound. This grapheme 'ui' for the long /oo/ sound is not that common although some of the word examples are common.

1. Word reading: Ask students to read each word carefully and tick to self-assess each word read. The words are *suit, fruit, juice, bruise, cruiser, recruit, suitor, juicy, grapefruit, suitable, sluice, lawsuit, recruitment* and *bruised*. Discuss any new or unusual word meanings.

2. Dictation time: Ask students to listen carefully and then write each sentence that you dictate.
a) We got fruit juice at the shop.   b) Next year we are going on a cruise ship.   c) I think I've done a suitable amount of homework this week.

3. Letter hunt: Ask students to scan through the text carefully and underline all the ui letters that are code for the long /oo/ sound. Then they should read the text, this time reading for accuracy and meaning. Ask a question to check understanding, for example: *Why was Louise's reaction sour?*

4. Now it's your turn: Ask students to write three of their own short sentences using at least one word per sentence that contains today's focus code.

Student Workbook 3 Lesson 25 ou as in soup

Warm up: Ask students to turn to the chart on page 4 and point to the letters that match the sound you say. Call out a selection of sounds from Chart 1 at a brisk pace, allowing just enough time for learners to scan and point to the letters each time.

Introduction: Explain to students that there are many graphemes which represent the long /oo/ sound including which 'ou' is a more unusual grapheme for this sound. Many of the example words have French origins.

1. Word reading: Ask students to read each word carefully and tick to self-assess each word read. The words are *you, soup, group, wound, route, troupe, rouge, coupé, recoup, mousse, coupon, soufflé, boulevard* and *bouffant*. Discuss any new or unusual word meanings.

2. Dictation time: Ask students to listen carefully and then write each sentence that you dictate.
a) We had chocolate mousse for pudding.   b) I used a coupon to save money.   c) The wound on my knee is almost better.

3. Letter hunt: Ask students to scan through the text carefully and underline all the ou letters that are code for the long /oo/ sound. Then they should read the text, this time reading for accuracy and meaning. Ask a question to check understanding, for example: *Why did the speaker take the longest route to the café?*

4. Now it's your turn: Ask students to write three of their own short sentences using at least one word per sentence that contains today's focus code.

Student Workbook 3 Lesson 26 o as in move

Warm up: Ask students to turn to the chart on page 4 and practise saying the sounds with a partner. One says the sounds in the shaded boxes, the other says the sounds in the white boxes, then swap.

Introduction: Explain to students that there are many graphemes which represent the long /oo/ sound. The grapheme 'o' for the long /oo/ sound is not that common although some of the word examples are common.

1. Word reading: Ask students to read each word carefully and tick to self-assess each word read. The words are *to, do, movie, lose, losing, move, moving, movable, remove, removal, improve, prove, disapprove* and *tomb*. Discuss any new or unusual word meanings.

2. Dictation time: Ask students to listen carefully and then write each sentence that you dictate.
a) We are moving to a new house on Monday.   b) I have been losing sleep recently.   c) I try hard to improve my maths skills.

3. Letter hunt: Ask students to scan through the text carefully and underline all the o letters that are code for the long /oo/ sound. Then they should read the text, this time reading for accuracy and meaning. Ask a question to check understanding, for example: *What did Mum's comment mean?*

4. Now it's your turn: Ask students to write three of their own short sentences using at least one word per sentence that contains today's focus code.

Student Workbook 3 Lesson 27 eu as in feud

Warm up: Ask students to turn to the chart on page 4 and point to the letters that match the sound you say. Call out a selection of sounds from Chart 1 at a brisk pace, allowing just enough time for learners to scan and point to the letters each time.

Introduction: Explain to students that there are many graphemes which represent the /yoo/ sound/. The grapheme eu for the /yoo/ sound is rare.

1. Word reading: Ask students to read each word carefully and tick to self-assess each word read. The words are *deuce, feud, neurotic, neutral, European, euphoria, pneumatic drill, pneumonia, feudal* and *neural*. Discuss any new or unusual word meanings.

2. Dictation time: Ask students to listen carefully and then write each sentence that you dictate.
a) Pneumonia is a horrid illness.   b) The pneumatic drill was very noisy.   c) I think we will have a European holiday this year.

3. Letter hunt: Ask students to scan through the text carefully and underline all the eu letters that are code for the /yoo/ sound. Then they should read the text, this time reading for accuracy and meaning. Ask a question to check understanding, for example: *What was Mavis upset about?*

4. Now it's your turn: Ask students to write three of their own short sentences using at least one word per sentence that contains today's focus code.

Student Workbook 3 Lesson 28 ew as in new

Warm up: Ask students to turn to the chart on page 4 and practise saying the sounds with a partner. One says the sounds in the shaded boxes, the other says the sounds in the white boxes, then swap.

Introduction: Explain to students that there are four main graphemes which represent the /yoo/ sound: u, ue, u-e and ew. Rarer graphemes for the /yoo/ sound include: eu and iew.

1. Word reading: Ask students to read each word carefully and tick to self-assess each word read. The words are *new, newt, knew, few, pew, dew, dewy, stew, sinew, mews, nephew, curfew, mildew, newborn* and *pewter*. Discuss any new or unusual word meanings.

2. Dictation time: Ask students to listen carefully and then write each sentence that you dictate.
a) We had vegetable stew for dinner.   b) My nephew is called Stewart.   c) Dad extended my curfew to nine o'clock.

3. Letter hunt: Ask students to scan through the text carefully and underline all the ew letters that are code for the /yoo/ sound. Then they should read the text, this time reading for accuracy and meaning. Ask a question to check understanding, for example: *What was Stewart and Roseanne's old home like?*

4. Now it's your turn: Ask students to write three of their own short sentences using at least one word per sentence that contains today's focus code.

Student Workbook 3 Lesson 29 iew as in view

Warm up: Ask students to turn to the chart on page 4 and point to the letters that match the sound you say. Call out a selection of sounds from Chart 1 at a brisk pace, allowing just enough time for learners to scan and point to the letters each time.

Introduction: Explain to students that there are four main graphemes which represent the /yoo/ sound: u, ue, u-e and ew. Rarer graphemes for the /yoo/ sound include: eu and iew. View is the root word for all 'iew' as /yoo/ words.

1. Word reading: Ask students to read each word carefully and tick to self-assess each word read. The words are *view, review, viewpoint, preview, viewing, viewfinder, viewed, overview, interview, interviewer* and *interviewee*. Discuss any new or unusual word meanings.

2. Dictation time: Ask students to listen carefully and then write each sentence that you dictate.
a) I have a job interview at the book shop.   b) The view from the top of the hill was stunning.
c) I wrote a detailed book review.

3. Letter hunt: Ask students to scan through the text carefully and underline all the iew letters that are code for the /yoo/ sound. Then they should read the text, this time reading for accuracy and meaning. Ask a question to check understanding, for example: *What does it mean to be a 'reviewer'?*

4. Now it's your turn: Ask students to write three of their own short sentences using at least one word per sentence that contains today's focus code.

Student Workbook 3 Lesson 30 ough as in thought

Warm up: Ask students to turn to the chart on page 5 and practise saying the sounds with a partner. One says the sounds in the shaded boxes, the other says the sounds in the white boxes, then swap.

Introduction: Explain to students that the grapheme 'ough' is a very rare spelling variation of the /or/ phoneme. Words such as 'ought', 'bought' and 'thought', however, are used very commonly.

1. Word reading: Ask students to read each word carefully and tick to self-assess each word read. The words are *ought, nought, fought, bought, brought, sought, thoughtful, thoughtless, thoughtfully* and *overwrought*. Discuss any new or unusual word meanings.

2. Dictation time: Ask students to listen carefully and then write each sentence that you dictate.
a) It was thoughtless to keep the door open.   b) I bought a new hoodie.   c) I sought advice from the customer service assistant.

3. Letter hunt: Ask students to scan through the text carefully and underline all the ough letters that are code for the /or/ sound. Then they should read the text, this time reading for accuracy and meaning. Ask a question to check understanding, for example: *What triggered Brian to change?*

4. Now it's your turn: Ask students to write three of their own short sentences using at least one word per sentence that contains today's focus code.

Student Workbook 3 Lesson 31 augh as in caught

Warm up: Ask students to turn to the chart on page 5 and point to the letters that match the sound you say. Call out a selection of sounds from Chart 2 at a brisk pace, allowing just enough time for learners to scan and point to the letters each time.

Introduction: Explain to students that the grapheme 'augh' is a very rare spelling variation of the /or/ phoneme. Words such as 'taught', 'caught' and 'daughter', however, are used very commonly.

1. Word reading: Ask students to read each word carefully and tick to self-assess each word read. The words are *taught, caught, fraught, daughter, haughty, distraught, naughty, naught, haughtily, naughtiness* and *untaught*. Discuss any new or unusual word meanings.

2. Dictation time: Ask students to listen carefully and then write each sentence that you dictate.
a) My sister taught me to paint nails.   b) My kitten is so naughty.   c) I was distraught when I lost my new pen.

3. Letter hunt: Ask students to scan through the text carefully and underline all the augh letters that are code for the /or/ sound. Then they should read the text, this time reading for accuracy and meaning. Ask a question to check understanding, for example: *Why did Patricia dread her daughter's visits?*

4. Now it's your turn: Ask students to write three of their own short sentences using at least one word per sentence that contains today's focus code.

Student Workbook 3 Lesson 32 ch as in school

Warm up: Ask students to turn to the chart on page 5 and practise saying the sounds with a partner. One says the sounds in the shaded boxes, the other says the sounds in the white boxes, then swap.

Introduction: Explain to students that the grapheme 'ch' is a less common spelling variation of the /k/ phoneme. The 'ch' spelling variation for /k/ has Greek origins.

1. Word reading: Ask students to read each word carefully and tick to self-assess each word read. The words are *school, chaos, anchor, chasm, orchid, chorus, scheme, chemist, chronic, chord, echo, stomach* and *arachnid*. Discuss any new or unusual word meanings.

2. Dictation time: Ask students to listen carefully and then write each sentence that you dictate.
a) The problem looked technical.   b) I think I want to be a mechanic.   c) My day has been chaotic.

3. Letter hunt: Ask students to scan through the text carefully and underline all the ch letters that are code for the /k/ sound. Then they should read the text, this time reading for accuracy and meaning. Ask a question to check understanding, for example: *What is archaeology?*

4. Now it's your turn: Ask students to write three of their own short sentences using at least one word per sentence that contains today's focus code.

Student Workbook 3 Lesson 33 qu as in bouquet

Warm up: Ask students to turn to the chart on page 5 and point to the letters that match the sound you say. Call out a selection of sounds from Chart 2 at a brisk pace, allowing just enough time for learners to scan and point to the letters each time.

Introduction: Explain to students that the grapheme 'qu' is a less common spelling variation of the /k/ phoneme. It has French origins as can be seen by other spelling features of the example words.

1. Word reading: Ask students to read each word carefully and tick to self-assess each word read. The words are *quiche, conquer, mosquito, piquant, marquetry, marquee, briquette, masquerade, croquette, etiquette* and *mannequin*. Discuss any new or unusual word meanings.

2. Dictation time: Ask students to listen carefully and then write each sentence that you dictate.
a) We made a cheese and onion quiche.   b) My teacher says that etiquette is important.
c) I am determined to conquer this puzzle.

3. Letter hunt: Ask students to scan through the text carefully and underline all the qu letters that are code for the /k/ sound. Then they should read the text, this time reading for accuracy and meaning. Ask a question to check understanding, for example: *How do you know whether a mosquito is female?*

4. Now it's your turn: Ask students to write three of their own short sentences using at least one word per sentence that contains today's focus code.

Student Workbook 3 Lesson 34 que as in plaque

Warm up: Ask students to turn to the chart on page 5 and practise saying the sounds with a partner. One says the sounds in the shaded boxes, the other says the sounds in the white boxes, then swap.

Introduction: Explain to students that the grapheme 'que' is a less common spelling variation of the /k/ phoneme. It has French origins as can be seen by other spelling features of the example words.

1. Word reading: Ask students to read each word carefully and tick to self-assess each word read. The words are *cheque, queue, clique, pique, picturesque, unique, plaque, brusque, boutique, oblique, technique, mosque* and *antique*. Discuss any new or unusual word meanings.

2. Dictation time: Ask students to listen carefully and then write each sentence that you dictate.
a) I checked my hair in the antique mirror.   b) My boots are customised and unique.   c) I like to shop in local boutiques.

3. Letter hunt: Ask students to scan through the text carefully and underline all the que letters that are code for the /k/ sound. Then they should read the text, this time reading for accuracy and meaning. Ask a question to check understanding, for example: *Which outfit does the speaker advise getting?*

4. Now it's your turn: Ask students to write three of their own short sentences using at least one word per sentence that contains today's focus code.

Student Workbook 3 Lesson 35 quar as in quarter

Warm up: Ask students to turn to the chart on page 5 and point to the letters that match the sound you say. Call out a selection of sounds from Chart 2 at a brisk pace, allowing just enough time for learners to scan and point to the letters each time.

Introduction: Explain to students that the grapheme 'qu' preceding the grapheme 'ar' alerts the reader to pronounce the 'ar' as the /or/ phoneme.

1. Word reading: Ask students to read each word carefully and tick to self-assess each word read. The words are *quart, quarter, quarterly, quartet, quarters, quarterfinal, quarterback* and *quartz*. Discuss any new or unusual word meanings.

2. Dictation time: Ask students to listen carefully and then write each sentence that you dictate.
a) I bought some quartz earrings.   b) The time is quarter past two.   c) Jim plays the position of quarterback.

3. Letter hunt: Ask students to scan through the text carefully and underline all the quar letters that are code for the /quor/ sound. Then they should read the text, this time reading for accuracy and meaning. Ask a question to check understanding, for example: *What did Ellen and Jamie quarrel about?*

4. Now it's your turn: Ask students to write three of their own short sentences using at least one word per sentence that contains today's focus code.

Student Workbook 3 Lesson 36 gue as in catalogue

Warm up: Ask students to turn to the chart on page 5 and practise saying the sounds with a partner. One says the sounds in the shaded boxes, the other says the sounds in the white boxes, then swap.

Introduction: Explain to students that the grapheme 'gue' is a less common spelling variation of the /g/ phoneme. It has French origins.

1. Word reading: Ask students to read each word carefully and tick to self-assess each word read. The words are *rogue, vogue, catalogue, intrigue, fatigue, plague, vaguely, colleagues, synagogue* and *league*. Discuss any new or unusual word meanings.

2. Dictation time: Ask students to listen carefully and then write each sentence that you dictate.
a) We used images from catalogues.   b) In cookery I learned how to make meringue.   c) I am intrigued about the new college.

3. Letter hunt: Ask students to scan through the text carefully and underline all the gue letters that are code for the /g/ sound. Then they should read the text, this time reading for accuracy and meaning. Ask a question to check understanding, for example: *Why was Victor flying to England ?*

4. Now it's your turn: Ask students to write three of their own short sentences using at least one word per sentence that contains today's focus code.

Student Workbook 3 Lesson 37 ine as in shine

Warm up: Ask students to turn to the chart on page 5 and point to the letters that match the sound you say. Call out a selection of sounds from Chart 2 at a brisk pace, allowing just enough time for learners to scan and point to the letters each time.

Introduction: Explain to students that the letter pattern 'ine' in some words can be decoded as straightforward split digraph 'i-e' with letter 'n' therefore pronounce /igh/+/n/.

1. Word reading: Ask students to read each word carefully and tick to self-assess each word read. The words are *shine, twine, alpine, canine, feline, define, saline, refine, turbine, mine, combine, declined, refinery* and *defined*. Discuss any new or unusual word meanings.

2. Dictation time: Ask students to listen carefully and then write each sentence that you dictate.
a) The popularity of the book declined over time.   b) My desk is made from pine.   c) I ran up a hill with a steep incline.

3. Letter hunt: Ask students to scan through the text carefully and underline all the ine letters that are code for the /igh/+/n/ sounds. Then they should read the text, this time reading for accuracy and meaning. Ask a question to check understanding, for example: *How many puppies were there?*

4. Now it's your turn: Ask students to write three of their own short sentences using at least one word per sentence that contains today's focus code.

Student Workbook 3 Lesson 38 ine as in engine

Warm up: Ask students to turn to the chart on page 5 and practise saying the sounds with a partner. One says the sounds in the shaded boxes, the other says the sounds in the white boxes, then swap.

Introduction: Explain to students that the letter pattern 'ine' in some words is pronounced as 'in' which is two phonemes: /i/ + /n/. The grapheme 'ne' is simply representing the /n/ phoneme.

1. Word reading: Ask students to read each word carefully and tick to self-assess each word read. The words are *engine, famine, masculine, genuine, feminine, medicine, determine, jasmine, examine, crinoline* and *intestine*. Discuss any new or unusual word meanings.

2. Dictation time: Ask students to listen carefully and then write each sentence that you dictate.
a) Jasmine is a fragrant flower.   b) I examined the cake carefully.   c) The bus had a problem with its engine.

3. Letter hunt: Ask students to scan through the text carefully and underline all the ine letters that are code for the /i/+/n/ sounds. Then they should read the text, this time reading for accuracy and meaning. Ask a question to check understanding, for example: *Why did the speaker go to the vet?*

4. Now it's your turn: Ask students to write three of their own short sentences using at least one word per sentence that contains today's focus code.

Student Workbook 3 Lesson 39 ine as in magazine

Warm up: Ask students to turn to the chart on page 5 and point to the letters that match the sound you say. Call out a selection of sounds from Chart 2 at a brisk pace, allowing just enough time for learners to scan and point to the letters each time.

Introduction: Explain to students that the letter pattern 'ine' has French origins and it is pronounced in some words as 'een' which is two phonemes: /ee/ + /n/.

1. Word reading: Ask students to read each word carefully and tick to self-assess each word read. The words are *magazine, gasoline, routine, sardines, submarine, ravine, machine, marine, limousine, vaccine, cuisine* and *pristine*. Discuss any new or unusual word meanings.

2. Dictation time: Ask students to listen carefully and then write each sentence that you dictate.
a) I play a tambourine in the band.   b) I keep my bedroom pristine.   c) I like to stick to a routine.

3. Letter hunt: Ask students to scan through the text carefully and underline all the ine letters that are code for the /ee/+/n/ sounds. Then they should read the text, this time reading for accuracy and meaning. Ask a question to check understanding, for example: *Why did the chauffeur go into the forecourt shop?*

4. Now it's your turn: Ask students to write three of their own short sentences using at least one word per sentence that contains today's focus code.

Student Workbook 3 Lesson 40 mn as in column

Warm up: Ask students to turn to the chart on page 5 and practise saying the sounds with a partner. One says the sounds in the shaded boxes, the other says the sounds in the white boxes, then swap.

Introduction: Explain to students that the grapheme 'mn' is a very rare spelling variation of the /m/ phoneme but words with this spelling are commonly used.

1. Word reading: Ask students to read each word carefully and tick to self-assess each word read. The words are *autumn, column, solemn, condemn, hymn, columnist, hymns* and *solemnly*. Discuss any new or unusual word meanings.

2. Dictation time: Ask students to listen carefully and then write each sentence that you dictate.
a) The old building was condemned.   b) The mourners at the funeral were solemn.   c) Autumn is the season of harvest.

3. Letter hunt: Ask students to scan through the text carefully and underline all the mn letters that are code for the /m/ sound. Then they should read the text, this time reading for accuracy and meaning. Ask a question to check understanding, for example: *What did the columnist write about?*

4. Now it's your turn: Ask students to write three of their own short sentences using at least one word per sentence that contains today's focus code.

Student Workbook 3 Lesson 41 ps as in pseudo

Warm up: Ask students to turn to the chart on page 5 and point to the letters that match the sound you say. Call out a selection of sounds from Chart 2 at a brisk pace, allowing just enough time for learners to scan and point to the letters each time.

Introduction: Explain to students that the grapheme 'ps' is a very rare spelling variation of the /s/ phoneme. It has Greek origins.

1. Word reading: Ask students to read each word carefully and tick to self-assess each word read. The words are *psalm, psyche, pseudonym, psychiatry, psychiatrist, psychology, psychologist, psoriasis, psychic* and *psychedelic*. Discuss any new or unusual word meanings.

2. Dictation time: Ask students to listen carefully and then write each sentence that you dictate.
a) I write books under a pseudonym.   b) I painted my room in psychedelic colours.   c) I would like to become a child psychologist.

3. Letter hunt: Ask students to scan through the text carefully and underline all the ps letters that are code for the /s/ sound. Then they should read the text, this time reading for accuracy and meaning. Ask a question to check understanding, for example: *Why does Joseph plan to use a pseudonym?*

4. Now it's your turn: Ask students to write three of their own short sentences using at least one word per sentence that contains today's focus code.

Student Workbook 3 Lesson 42 al(m) as in palm

Warm up: Ask students to turn to the chart on page 5 and practise saying the sounds with a partner. One says the sounds in the shaded boxes, the other says the sounds in the white boxes, then swap.

Introduction: Explain to students that the grapheme 'al' is a very rare spelling of the /ar/ phoneme. Some words with this spelling variation, however, are used commonly.

1. Word reading: Ask students to read each word carefully and tick to self-assess each word read. The words are *alms, almshouse, psalm, palm, balm, calm, embalm, almond, qualms, halfway, behalf, calves* and *halves*. Discuss any new or unusual word meanings.

2. Dictation time: Ask students to listen carefully and then write each sentence that you dictate.
a) Classical music helps me to feel calm.   b) I like warm, balmy evenings.   c) The farm had lots of new calves.

3. Letter hunt: Ask students to scan through the text carefully and underline all the al letters that are code for the /ar/ sound. Then they should read the text, this time reading for accuracy and meaning. Ask a question to check understanding, for example: *Why did the dog warn the people off?*

4. Now it's your turn: Ask students to write three of their own short sentences using at least one word per sentence that contains today's focus code.

Student Workbook 3 Lesson 43 a(lt) as in salt

Warm up: Ask students to turn to the chart on page 5 and point to the letters that match the sound you say. Call out a selection of sounds from Chart 2 at a brisk pace, allowing just enough time for learners to scan and point to the letters each time.

Introduction: Explain to students that the letter pattern 'alt' alerts the reader that the letter 'a' might be pronounced as an /o/ sound.

1. Word reading: Ask students to read each word carefully and tick to self-assess each word read. The words are *halt, malt, salt, exalt, halter, falter, paltry, alter, basalt, cobalt, altar, altruistic, Malta, Maltese* and *alternating*. Discuss any new or unusual word meanings.

2. Dictation time: Ask students to listen carefully and then write each sentence that you dictate.
a) I exercise on alternate days.   b) I did not falter in my French exam.   c) It isn't healthy to have too much salt in your diet.

3. Letter hunt: Ask students to scan through the text carefully and underline all the a letters that are code for the /o/ sound. Then they should read the text, this time reading for accuracy and meaning. Ask a question to check understanding, for example: *Why was the speaker dancing a waltz?*

4. Now it's your turn: Ask students to write three of their own short sentences using at least one word per sentence that contains today's focus code.

Student Workbook 3 Lesson 44 ture as in picture

Warm up: Ask students to turn to the chart on page 5 and practise saying the sounds with a partner. One says the sounds in the shaded boxes, the other says the sounds in the white boxes, then swap.

Introduction: Explain to students that the letter pattern 'ture' in the example words can be pronounced close to a /ch/ phoneme followed by a schwa: "chu". A schwa is an unstressed syllable.

1. Word reading: Ask students to read each word carefully and tick to self-assess each word read. The words are *picture, capture, future, nature, pastures, fixtures, gesture, culture, venture, temperature, stature, fracture* and *mixture*. Discuss any new or unusual word meanings.

2. Dictation time: Ask students to listen carefully and then write each sentence that you dictate.
a) I like to watch adventure movies.   b) I try to capture the light in my pictures.   c) It was a kind gesture to give flowers to the cook.

3. Letter hunt: Ask students to scan through the text carefully and underline all the ture letters that are code for the /chu/ sound. Then they should read the text, this time reading for accuracy and meaning. Ask a question to check understanding, for example: *Which creature did the speaker like the most?*

4. Now it's your turn: Ask students to write three of their own short sentences using at least one word per sentence that contains today's focus code.

Student Workbook 3 Lesson 45 eau as in beauty

Warm up: Ask students to turn to the chart on page 5 and point to the letters that match the sound you say. Call out a selection of sounds from Chart 2 at a brisk pace, allowing just enough time for learners to scan and point to the letters each time.

Introduction: Explain to students that the grapheme 'eau' can represent two main sounds: /yoo/ as in 'beauty' and /oa/ as in 'beau'. The grapheme 'eau' is pronounced /o/ in the word 'bureaucracy'.

1. Word reading: Ask students to read each word carefully and tick to self-assess each word read. The words are *beauty, beautify, beautiful, beautician, beautifully, chateau, beau, bureau, plateau, tableau* and *trousseau*. Discuss any new or unusual word meanings.

2. Dictation time: Ask students to listen carefully and then write each sentence that you dictate.
a) I want to be a beautician when I leave school.   b) We stayed in a chateau in France.   c) My grades have reached a plateau.

3. Letter hunt: Ask students to scan through the text carefully and underline all the eau letters. Then they should read the text, this time reading for accuracy and meaning. Ask a question to check understanding, for example: *Who is Francis?*

4. Now it's your turn: Ask students to write three of their own short sentences using at least one word per sentence that contains today's focus code.

Student Workbook 3 Lesson 46 re as in theatre

Warm up: Ask students to turn to the chart on page 5 and practise saying the sounds with a partner. One says the sounds in the shaded boxes, the other says the sounds in the white boxes, then swap.

Introduction: Explain to students that there may be some variation of spelling of words with the grapheme 're'. In these words, 're' is pronounced as a schwa /u/. In the USA some words may be spelt with 'er' instead of 're'.

1. Word reading: Ask students to read each word carefully and tick to self-assess each word read. The words are *centre, metre, litre, fibre, ogre, theatre, mediocre, acre, goitre, timbre, sceptre, ochre, lucre, sabre* and *meagre*. Discuss any new or unusual word meanings.

2. Dictation time: Ask students to listen carefully and then write each sentence that you dictate.

a) I feel like my work is mediocre.   b) I have written a story about an ogre.   c) I read a book about a sabretooth tiger.

3. Letter hunt: Ask students to scan through the text carefully and underline all the re letters that are code for the schwa /u/ sound. Then they should read the text, this time reading for accuracy and meaning. Ask a question to check understanding, for example: *What did the ogre use for his sabre?*

4. Now it's your turn: Ask students to write three of their own short sentences using at least one word per sentence that contains today's focus code.

Student Workbook 3 Lesson 47 Word level assessment

Word reading: Listen to students read each of the words.

ghastly	system	great	quarrel	nourish
review	mission	threw	disobey	coupon
design	fracture	sphere	grief	warden
column	swatch	cookies	casual	parsley
devious	listen	naughty	catalogue	feisty
straight	removal	upfront	weight	tough

Word dictation: Dictate these words for students to write.

1. passion	11. enough	21. gnome
2. money	12. pigeon	22. neutral
3. confusion	13. gherkin	23. rustle
4. freebie	14. sewage	24. curfew
5. famous	15. wash	25. convey
6. crystal	16. juice	26. fought
7. curious	17. squat	27. eighty
8. niece	18. route	28. daughter
9. photograph	19. warmth	29. greatly
10. heist	20. moving	30. anchor

Student Workbook 3 Lesson 48 Text level assessment

Text reading: Listen to students read the passage or ask them to read to a partner and self-assess their confidence in reading the passage.

The editor of the magazine called for an urgent review. She was not happy about the pictures chosen for the autumn season's main column. "Your mission is to sort this chaos out!" she hollered at the chief designer. "The photographs aren't straight. The breaks aren't in the right places. Get a crew together and get working immediately."

The chief designer called a meeting with his team. They brought in ghostwriters to rework some of the article text. They allocated a quarter page for the best visuals they could find. It took eighteen hours of solid work – including through the night – to get the magazine up to the standard that was expected.

"What a ghastly job that was!" laughed the team afterwards. "Like something out of a movie or a theatre production!"

"Good job we operate like a smooth engine," congratulated the chief designer.

The editor was thrilled with the final quality and apologised if she had caused any internal feuds. "This magazine is so precious to me," she explained, "I'm sorry for being a bureaucrat but we need to get it right or we'd get cancelled."

Text dictation: Dictate this passage for students to write.

Sasha laughed with excitement. She had qualified for admission to the new college after she finished school. She had studied straight through the holiday breaks and now she had passed eight exams. To celebrate she watched a movie about a theatre haunted by a ghost. Her family would be moving across town. She would miss her crew, but it was only a quarter of an hour away. The new house was beautiful.

The English Alphabetic Code Chart

sounds	simple code	complex code (spelling alternatives)						
/s/	s snake	ss glass	ce palace	se house	c (e i y) city	sc scissors	st castle	ps pseudonym
/a/	a apple							
/t/	t tent	tt letter	ed skipped					
/i/	i insect	y cymbals						
/p/	p pan	pp puppet						
/n/	n net	nn bonnet	kn knot	gn gnome	ne engine			
/k/	k kit	c cat	ck duck	ch chameleon	qu bouquet	que plaque		
/e/	e egg	ea head	ai said					
/h/	h hat	wh who						
/r/	r rat	rr arrow	wr write	rh rhinoceros				
/m/	m map	mm hammer	me welcome	mb thumb	mn column			
/d/	d dig	dd puddle	ed rained					
/g/	g girl	gg juggle	gu guitar	gh ghost	gue catalogue			
/o/	o octopus	(w)a watch	(qu)a qualify	a(lt) salt				
/u/	u umbrella	o son	ou touch	ough thorough				
/l/	l ladder	ll shell						
/ul/	le kettle	il pencil	al hospital	el camel				
/f/	f feather	ff cliff	ph photograph	gh laugh				
/b/	b bat	bb rabbit	bu building					
/j/	j jug	ge cabbage	g (e i y) giraffe	dge Fridge				
/y/	y yawn							
/ai/	ai aid	ay tray	a table	ae sundae	a-e cake			
	ey prey	ea break	eigh eight	aigh straight				
/w/	w web	wh wheel	u penguin					
/oa/	oa oak	ow bow	o yo-yo	oe oboe	o-e rope	ough dough	eau plateau	

/igh/	**igh** night	**ie** tie	**i** behind	**y** fly	**i-e** bike	**ei** eider	**eye** eye	
/ee/	**ee** eel	**ea** eat	**e** emu	**e-e** concrete	**ey** key	**ie** chief	**i(ne)** sardine	
/i-ee/	**y** sunny	**ey** monkey	**ie** movie					
/or/	**or** fork	**oar** oars	**oor** door	**ore** snore	**our** four	**(w)ar** wardrobe	**(qu)ar** quarter	**(w)a** water
	aw dawn	**au** sauce	**al** chalk	**augh** caught	**ough** thought			
/z/	**z** zebra	**zz** jazz	**s** fries	**se** cheese	**ze** breeze			
/ng/	**ng** gong	**n** jungle		/ngk/	**nk** ink	**nc** uncle		
/v/	**v** violin	**ve** dove						
short /oo/	**oo** book	**oul** should	**u** push					
long /oo/	**oo** moon	**ue** blue	**u-e** flute	**ew** crew	**ui** fruit	**ou** soup	**o** move	**ough** through
/ks/	**x** fox	**ks** books	**cks** ducks	**kes** cakes		/gz/	**x** exam	**gs** pegs
/ch/	**ch** chairs	**tch** patch		/chu/	**ture** picture			
/sh/	**sh** sheep	**ch** chef	**ti** station	**ci** magician	**ssi** admission			
unvoiced /th/	**th** thistle		voiced /th/	**th** there				
/kw/	**qu** queen							
/ou/	**ou** ouch	**ow** owl	**ough** plough					
/oi/	**oi** ointment	**oy** toy						
/yoo/	**ue** statue	**u** unicorn	**u-e** tube	**ew** new	**eu** pneumatic			
/er/	**er** mermaid	**ir** birthday	**ur** nurse	**ear** earth	**(w)or** world			
schwa /er/ (uh)	**er** mixer	**our** humour	**re** theatre	**ar** collar	**or** sailor			
/ar/	**ar** artist	**a** father	**al(m)** palm	**al(f)** half	**al(ves)** calves			
/air/	**air** hair	**are** hare	**ear** bear	**ere** where				
/eer/	**eer** deer	**ear** ears	**ere** adhere	**ier** cashier				
/zh/	**si** television	**s** treasure	**z** azure	**g** courgette	**ge** collage			

First published by Blackberry Cottage Ltd, UK 2020-04-24

Print ISBN: 978-1691508891

www.abigailsteel.com

With credit, acknowledgement and thanks to Debbie Hepplewhite, MBE.
www.alphabeticcodecharts.com
www.phonicsinternational.com

With thanks to Academies Enterprise Trust for their forward thinking, inclusive approaches and passion for children to choose remarkable lives.

Printed in Great Britain
by Amazon

37331993R00051